JAY'S

VIRTUAL

Pub Quiz Book

By Jay Flynn

MB

MIRROR BOOKS

First published by Mirror Books in 2020

Mirror Books is part of Reach plc
10 Lower Thames Street
London EC3R 6EN

www.mirrorbooks.co.uk

Print ISBN 978-1-913406-40-0
eBook ISBN 978-1-913406-43-1

Printed and bound in Great Britain by
CPI Group (UK) Ltd, Croydon, CR0 4YY

A CIP catalogue record for this book is available from the British Library.

1 3 5 7 9 10 8 6 4 2

For Christopher Earl Cantwell Esq: My Grandfather,
my guiding light, my inspiration, and 22 years on
I hope that you are still proud of everything I do.

To my son Jack, you were too young to understand
these crazy times we lived in, but always follow
your dreams, I will always have your back.

Contents

Foreword

"I do accept that what we're doing is extraordinary: we're taking away the ancient, inalienable right of free-born people of the United Kingdom to go to the pub, and I can understand how people feel about that,… It's a huge wrench".

The words of Boris Johnson, British Prime Minister, March 2020, at the start of what was about to become months of lockdown. Luckily for us, we had Jay Flynn, a former pub landlord from Lancashire who dreaded losing his right to his weekly quiz at his local pub, his chance to connect with friends and forget about the week. So he created a virtual pub quiz. It was then that Jay became something of a lockdown hero.

My name is Alex Holmes, but if you've played #JaysVirtualPubQuiz you probably know me as "the man, the myth, the legend that is the wonderful Alex standing by on social media" (Jay's words not mine), but you can just call me Alex. I am first and foremost a fan and player of the quiz, but it was in week 2 that I reached out to Jay who I didn't know and offered my help and support.

My day job is Deputy CEO at The Diana Award (a youth charity with an award, mentoring and anti-bullying programme) where I head up our fundraising, development and partnerships. I, like many others, was facing lockdown thinking, how will I deal with an indefinite time inside my home? I found the quiz like many others randomly on Facebook, I and my friends were hooked from my first attempt. It was clear that Jay was onto something special and I wanted to see how I might be able to support him, as I felt he must be overwhelmed.

After a quick direct message to his inbox with a few ideas: a hashtag for social media (everyone loved the quiz and was telling the world on their social media about it, but this resulted in many different hashtags being created, so I suggested #JaysVirtualPubQuiz and it's become our trending weekly hit), publicity/press (I felt the world needed to know about the quiz, so set about contacting journalists and before we knew it we were in Washington Post, on national TV news bulletins and shows and almost every major national print, radio & TV show) and lastly partnerships (like my success of reaching out to Jay, I was always good at this, and helped us strike up relationships and partnerships with, the likes of YouTube/Google HQ team, Stephen Fry, many charities and even some brands along the way to truly help Jay turn this into a career.

Seeing how Jay and the quiz has brought together families, friends and colleagues has been nothing short of thrilling. We've heard stories of lonely feeling less lonely thanks to quiz, of families with teenagers bonding thanks to the quiz and thanks to technology connecting with families abroad, and of course we are now approaching having raised £1 million pounds for charity. A real memory is persuading Gary Barlow to perform in the half-time break and then seeing on social media this concert play out in over 170,000 households across the nation, with most households having up to 3 people in them. This was HUGE. I always joke it's one of Gary's biggest concerts, and the best thing was, it was free. YouTube and Google headquarters gave us stats at one point that showed over half of online quizzes' traffic/views was coming from Jay's Virtual Pub Quiz.

Having headed up a lot of our interaction with players on social media, I have been delighted to see the response. Jay has been turned into a scarecrow at a Norfolk local scarecrow festival, made into a ceramic art miniature scene and featured in a wide arrange of memes as tributes, and I loved our Saturday night fancy dress theme of "dress like Jay", which provided many laughs.

Jay has a unique ability to connect with 6 to 60-year-olds, he is warm, down to earth and makes mistakes just like all of us, and he hasn't once tired in the weeks he's been busily creating this for us all.

Being a part of this in what was an unprecedented time for the country is one of the achievements I am most proud of in my life. It's been lovely to use some of my charity skills to aid the quiz but mostly it's been great just to be a nice human and help Jay out.

Jay and I still haven't met each other yet, we are virtual friends, but I know I have a friend for life. Just like many of you reading this, it feels like Jay is a friend, a trusted and regular visitor in your living room, the friend who can entertain you and the people most important in your life, and he never lets us down.

I'm excited to see and hear your stories of how YOU have become Jay, the quizmaster in your household, friends or work group, so as always, please do get in touch on our social media and use #JaysVirtualPubQuiz. I hope this book and your hosting brings as much joy as it has brought Jay and me.

Alex

Introduction

Hello! You have in your hands a quiz book that, had it not been for the events on Friday March 20th 2020, would never have existed.

Let me introduce myself! My name is Jay Flynn and I am the creator, writer and presenter of Jay's Virtual Pub Quiz. At the beginning of March my business partner and I handed back the keys to a pub we had been running for just over a year, but having tried everything we could, we were always fighting a losing battle. The best night of the week by far was Thursday night. Each week I would host a quiz for anywhere between 30-40 people, and they were so much fun. The teams and I would have banter all night, my mistakes would be picked up on quickly and talked about for weeks after. I was devastated to no longer be able to host the quiz for the teams, but it meant I could also return to being on the other side of the microphone and reunite with the team I have played with for over three years.

And then came the announcement on 20th March that the pubs were being ordered to close. I could see that this would be a long closure and my heart went out to everyone who was in the licensed trade. I knew what times were like when trade was tough. This was a whole new level, and I got thinking about my friends I quizzed with and quiz teams I had played against in various pubs in town. It was as I sat bored the following day that I had an idea. What if I could host a quiz online that everyone could play along with? So without even contemplating how to achieve this or how many people might be interested in the idea, I created an event on my personal Facebook page, set the date for 26th March at 8pm and left it there for friends to look at and share if they wanted to. And then I forgot about it.

Monday lunchtime I received a message on Facebook in the request box from someone I had never heard of and had no mutual friends with, asking me how this quiz was going to work. I was confused - how did this person know about it? I checked the event for the first time and it showed 800 people interested. My boss Ian joked that it would be 1,000 people, by the time we went home. How wrong we were. By 7pm it had reached 10,000 people and by the time I completed the 20-minute drive home it had hit over 20,000 people interested. At 8pm The Prime Minister declared a total lockdown of the UK, and that was when it truly took off. By the time the first quiz went live there were over 500,000 people interested in the quiz.

Straight away there were problems. How on earth was I going to do this? All current technology was out of the window as there wasn't anything out there capable of handling the numbers involved! But also I had never tried to stream anything on the internet before! How on earth do you set a quiz for that many people with differing ages and IQ levels? I stuck with what I knew from years of hosting quizzes. Keep it simple and keep the questions fun and entertaining, where if people don't know the answer they might just learn something. At the end of the first quiz I asked anyone who wanted it to continue to join the Facebook page I had created (in the right way this time) and let their friends and families know to join in. The rest is history!

But it hadn't always been this way. As most people found out and some of my closest friends for the very first time, 10 years before all of this I had been homeless for two years on the streets of London. Only my closest circle of friends knew where I had come from, as there is a lot of stigma around homeless people. I was the exact definition of one at that time. I was a person, without a home. I wasn't an alcoholic, I wasn't a drug addict. I just didn't have anywhere to live. And that was my life for two years. I called my bench on Victoria Embankment my home (number three Riverside View) and set about an endless cycle of, well, nothingness. For two years I hardly spoke to anyone other than lost tourists looking for directions or drunk people on a night out trying to find their way home. Again, because I was always afraid of people's response to homeless people I always tried to blend in. I made sure to go to my "home" as late after midnight as possible and always tried to be away before the commuters arrived the following morning. The only company I kept was a mini digital radio on which I listened to the Chris Moyles Show on BBC Radio 1 every weekday morning to feel a part of something. I spent my time walking the streets every day, looking for lost change in the gutters or, on rare occasions, paper money. I survived on a diet of custard creams because at the time you could pick them up in the supermarkets for between 18-25p! I would save money wherever I could. Charity shops for bargain new clothes became my friend when something was wearing out. Trade-offs would always be made between food and essentials, and though I told myself that walking up to 18 hours a day on some occasions was my job, it didn't pay very well, some days not at all. So I always had to make sure I was planning ahead. There were days when I couldn't be bothered anymore. I hit the lowest ever moments of depression and when I got there and thought I couldn't sink any lower I found new ways to do it. I got punched in the face by a random stranger in an unprovoked attack. I overslept one morning and was woken up from my sleeping bag by a group of tourist kids throwing rocks at me. I woke up one morning covered in snow developing a cold I couldn't shake off for nearly three months. But through all those dark moments, through all those moments when I couldn't carry on, there was always something pulling me back from the brink. I once helped a lady out who was being harassed and followed by a very indecent guy. I stopped a group of young girls getting into an illegal taxi at a time where people were getting attacked. I stayed with a guy who had collapsed, and with First Aid knowledge put him into the recovery position while everyone around stared and watched. I watched the kindest gentleman ever run by me every morning. We would nod at each other. One morning he stopped, pulled a £10 note out and told me to get a coffee on him. I said that was way too much, would he like the change - and he told me to keep it. That's just some of the things that kept me going, and that doesn't even scratch the surface. It's been well covered over the lockdown period how the team at The Connections at St Martin's helped me. I will be forever in their debt and was so pleased with the amount of money that the incredible community raised for them. But if anyone had said when I walked through their famous Red Door 10 years ago that I would be writing the introduction to my very own Quiz book, I would have said they were delusional! They asked me what career I really wanted, and thanks to listening to them for two years, I wanted to produce radio shows!

10 years on and I am in a completely different place now, although the scars are still there. Having moved from London to the North West, I made new friends for life. But I still have trouble trusting people and letting people help me. Having spent two years doing everything for myself it's very hard to ask for help. But I've got an amazing group of people around me that

I'm proud to say have always got my back, and they know I will always have theirs, even if we don't get to see each other much. I'm married to Sarah and we have the most amazing three-year-old named Jack.

Being thrust into some kind of spotlight has been a very strange experience that I haven't been trained for. Having people recognise me whilst just out shopping or people sending messages asking for an autograph is just insane and something I don't think I will ever get used to. But as I keep getting told, it shows the impact the quizzes have had. They have brought families and friends together not just from here in the UK but across the world, and it is so heart-warming the amount of money that the community has raised for charity. When anyone asks what the best part of all of this has been, that is number 1 without a doubt.

There have been some truly pinch myself moments receiving the points of light award from Boris Johnson, the silver subscriber button from YouTube and of course the Guinness World Record for - most watched live quiz on YouTube. I have got to speak to Rick Astley, Gary Barlow and Maverick Sabre, who have performed on my quiz! And Stephen Fry, Jonathan Ross and Scarlet Moffatt have all hosted quizzes under my name. I have presented my own shortened version of the quiz live on Zoe Ball's Breakfast Show every Thursday morning, and now of course this book that you are holding in your hands right now.

If you have got this far reading this introduction, I want to say thank you so much. If you have been with us from week one or if you have just seen this on the shelf and bought it, THANK YOU. This book has just become the new starting point of many more exciting things to come.

Stay Safe

Jay

Top Tips for Hosting a Quiz

The hardest part of running any quiz is the questions. Researching and writing questions is the part that takes the longest, and no matter how many times you check the answers, mistakes will always occur. Actually hosting a quiz is a piece of cake, so to help you make your quiz night go as smoothly as possible, here are my top tips to get you going.

Get the right format. On the live quizzes I settled into a format of 50 questions split over five rounds. It allowed for the perfect balance of categories and difficulty level, without being too short or too long. But every quiz night could be different. The book is laid out in the live quiz format of 50-question quizzes, but you might want to have 100 questions or maybe fewer than 50. As the host, you decide!

Know your audience! There is no point turning up with 50 questions on sport, if your audience don't know their Andy Murrays from their Lewis Hamiltons! Tailor your quiz to your audience to keep them engaged.

Prepare! Once you have your format and know your audience, read through your questions. Check your answers, and be comfortable with word pronunciations.

Sounds obvious, but make sure you have pens and paper.

Confidence. Confidence. Confidence. When hosting the actual quiz, have confidence. Deliver each one as if you believe in it, and don't fear the banter that will come back to you. Make jokes and put everyone at ease, but as the quiz master, stay in control.

Be the ringmaster. As the host, you are the ringmaster, you are in charge. The quizmaster is always right! Even if they are blue in the face that they are right, your decision is final.

Have fun! It is a great feeling when you get to that final answer, seeing the winning team celebrate, but the losing teams' determinatio to win next time makes it also worthwhile!

You'll always learn something new. Whether you are hosting a quiz, playing a quiz, or just reading the questions in the book for fun, it adds to our knowledge. You might not necessarily know the answer to every question, otherwise you'd be a genius with an IQ over 200. But that new random fact you've learnt might just help in the future.

Now you're ready, go get 'em. Happy Quizzing - Love Jay.

Quiz 1

This is the quiz where it all began, Thursday March 26th 2020 and the first ever Jay's Virtual Pub Quiz. Watched by over 200,000 people on both Facebook and YouTube.

ROUND 1: SCIENCE AND NATURE

1. What is the largest internal organ in the human body?

2. How many wings does a mosquito have?

3. Approx. what percentage of the earth's surface is covered by water, 61%, 71% or 81%?

4. On which continent do giraffes live in the world?

5. Which English computer scientist is credited with inventing the world wide web?

6. In which year was Concorde officially retired?

7. What came first, the Zip or Velcro?

8. What is the Fahrenheit equivalent of 100 degrees Celsius?

ROUND 3: MUSIC

1. Westlife broke the record of singles from a debut artist with 7 in a row, but who stopped them getting number 8?

2. What is the biggest selling album of all time in the UK?

3. Lewis Capaldi wanted someone to know, have and hold in which song?

4. Which group released We Built This City in 1985?

5. Which country do AC/DC hail from?

6. Which was the first single of The Kinks to reach number 1 in the UK?

7. In which song did Elton John have his bags packed, pre-flight at 9am?

8. The Clash were formed in which UK City?

9. Who won the first ever Pop Idol?

10. Elton John's Candle in the Wind is recognised as the biggest selling physical single of all time. But which song is recognised as the best selling digital only single?

ROUND 4: HISTORY
NAME THE YEAR WHEN:

1. Princess Diana was born?

2. The Channel Tunnel opened?

3. Winston Churchill became Prime Minister for the first time?

4. The Millennium Dome was officially opened?

5. Channel 4 launched across the UK?

6. A bomb exploded below the north tower of the World Trade Centre in New York?

7. The first motorway the Preston bypas opened?

8. Her Majesty Queen Elizabeth was coronated?

9. London hosted the Olympics for the third time?

10. The Royal Air Force was founded?

ROUND 5: GENERAL KNOWLEDGE

1. Which UK Football club remains the only side to win the FA Cup whilst being a non-league side?

2. Which 2-person board game has 12 triangles called points on each side of the board?

3. Which politician served as London Mayor between 2008 and 2016?

4. What is the tallest building in the UK outside of London?

5. What is the third oldest university in the UK after Oxford and Cambridge?

6. What is the tallest mountain in the UK?

7. Gavin and Stacey was set in Essex and which Welsh town?

8. Located in Gateshead, what is 66ft (20 metres) Tall with wings of 177ft (54 metres) wide?

9. What was the most-searched thing on Google in 2019?

10. The current world record for an online quiz according to the Guinness World Record books stands at 16, 162 or 1622 people?

ANAGRAM

Name the British film
star from the anagram:
BRAIDS LIE

CRYPTIC CLUE

Name the London train
station from the cryptic clue:
Ruler is angry

LINKS

What links the following:
**Athens, Paris, St Louis,
London**

Did You Know?

If you lift a kangaroo's
tail off the ground, it
can't hop.

Quiz 2

ROUND 1: ENTERTAINMENT

1. Stormzy teamed up with which singer for the 2019 hit Take Me Back to London?

2. Martin Clunes starred as Colin Sutton in which ITV Drama?

3. Dude, Where's My Donkey, was the tagline to which trilogy-finishing movie comedy?

4. Who sang that they were too sexy in 1991?

5. Lucas North, Adam Carter and Tom Quinn were lead actors in which BBC drama?

6. Who played Truman Burbank in The Truman Show?

7. Who teamed up with Cliff Richard for a cover of Living Doll in 1986?

8. Complete the children's TV show title, Mighty Morphin...?

9. What was the name of the high school in Grease?

10. Bye Bye Baby was a 1975 hit for which group?

ROUND 2: SCIENCE AND NATURE

1. What does the E stand for in EMP?

2. Kr is the chemical symbol for which element?

3. Which dog breed is considered to have the highest IQ?

4. MMR stands for Measles, Mups and what?

5. Is a jellyfish classed as an animal or a plant?

6. Who is credited with the discovery of penicillin?

7. What is the more common name for the clavicle bone?

8. What is a baby koala called?

9. What name is given to a heart specialist?

10. Can a tiger retract its claws?

ROUND 3: FOOD AND DRINK

1. What is another name for zucchini?

2. What colour is Crème de Menthe?

3. What type of animal is an anchovy?

4. Budweiser originates in which country?

5. What is a dumb waiter?

6. What is Port Salut?

7. Which spirit is Pimm's based on?

8. A la Florentine is related to which leafy green edible plant?

9. Steak Tartare is served how?

10. A bad egg will do what in water?

ROUND 4: SPORT

1. The Potters is the nickname of which football club?

2. What legendary umpire Dickie Bird's first name?

3. Bjorn Borg was the first Swede to win which men's singles title?

4. In F1, who was known as The Professor?

5. Complete the NFL Team Name: New England...?

6. Rory Underwood was the first player to reach 50 international appearances in which sport?

7. How many points is the pink ball worth in snooker?

8. Eddie the Eagle was famous for finishing last in which event?

9. A velodrome hosts what type of sport?

10. Mike Tyson was fined $3 milion dollars in 1997 because he bit whose ear?

ROUND 5: GEBERAL KNOWLEDGE

1. The Dog in the Pond was a pub in which soap?

2. Which company bought the internet phone service Skype in 2011?

3. Saying the name of which Shakespearean play in theatre is said to be unlucky?

4. Complete the saying: A problem shared is a problem...?

5. MMIX is which number in Roman numerals?

6. Which vowel does not appear on the top line of a keyboard?

7. Harvard, Yale and Princeton are American types of what?

8. George is the name typically given to which part of an aircraft?

9. Sir Andrew Lloyd Webber and which other person wrote the musical Evita?

10. What was the name of the coffee shop in Friends?

ANAGRAM

Name the 2010 film
from the anagram:
SKETCHING SHEEP

CRYPTIC CLUE

Name the high street brand
from the cryptic clue:
Not at all wet

LINKS

What links the following:
**Desmond Tutu, Al
Gore, Malala Yousafzai,
Barack Obama**

Did You Know?

The only countries in
the world where you
can't buy Coca-Cola are
North Korea and Cuba.

Quiz 3

ROUND 1: ENTERTAINMENT

1. Adam and the Ants sang about Prince who in 1981?

2. Ashes to Ashes was the sequel to which TV series?

3. What was the name of the King of Duloc in Shrek?

4. Hello was the lead single from which singer's album in 2015?

5. Who played the title role in Lovejoy?

6. Tokyo Drift was a film in which movie franchise?

7. Sound of The Underground was a debut hit for which girl group?

8. Karen, Jake and Ben were the children in which TV comedy?

9. Reborn and Strikes Again are the second and third movies in which British spy comedy movie?

10. American Pie was a seventies hit for which artist?

ROUND 2: SCIENCE AND NATURE

1. Fe is the chemical symbol for which element?

2. Which planet has the most moons?

3. How many ventricles are in the human heart?

4. What is the other name for the Abominable Snowman?

5. The Latin name orca relates to which animal?

6. What is the name of the carnivorous plant native to the wetlands of the east coast of the USA?

7. Which flower is said to represent love?

8. Eskimos have traditionally had which breed of dog?

9. What is the other name for the Northern Lights?

10. A group of geese is called what?

ROUND 3: FOOD AND DRINK

1. Devils on Horseback is traditionally prunes wrapped in what?

2. Mendoza is a wine region in which country?

3. What is the main ingredient of Paella?

4. What does the acronym UHT stand for when related to milk?

5. Pistachios are fruits - True or False?

6. What type of oranges are used to make Marmalade?

7. True or false, the Hawaiian pizza originated in Hawaii?

8. Grenadine comes from which fruit?

9. Mycophobia is the fear of which food?

10. Pecorino cheese comes from which country?

ROUND 4: SPORT

1. What number becomes between 19 and 17 on a darts board?

2. Charlotte Brew was the first woman to ride in which horse race?

3. Who won his first F1 world championship on the last lap in 2008?

4. Hockey lasts how many minutes per match?

5. Which sport is played on a court 9.75 metres long and 6.4 metres wide?

6. Who holds the record for the most England caps in football?

7. In yards, what is the distance between wickets in cricket?

8. True or false, finishing 4th-8th in the Olympics gets you a diploma?

9. Flushing Meadows is the location for which tennis tournament?

10. Cross- country skiing and rifle shooting combine in which sport?

ROUND 5: GEBERAL KNOWLEDGE

1. The source of the Danube river is found in which country?

2. What is the second hardest stone after diamonds?

3. Who was the mother of Richard the Lionheart?

4. What is the lightest planet in terms of mass?

5. V is what number in Roman numerals?

6. What colour is the District Line on a London Underground map?

7. The Hula is a dance performed for tourists where?

8. Which canal runs between the Atlantic and Pacific oceans?

9. Winston Churchill died in which year?

10. The road to hell is paved with what according to the proverb?

ANAGRAM

Name the country and its capital city from the anagram:

BLINDED URINAL

CRYPTIC CLUE

Name the singer and rapper from the cryptic clue:

Very small tantrum

LINKS

What links the following:

Meg, Jo, Beth, Amy

Did You Know?

Bananas are curved because they grow towards the sun.

Quiz 4

ROUND 1: ENTERTAINMENT

1. Complete the movie title: Monty Python and the Meaning of...?

2. Slow Hands was a 2017 hit for which artist?

3. General Lee was the name of the car in which TV series?

4. Tom Hanks and Tim Allen provided voices in which children's animated film series?

5. Which former Soldier Soldier actors sung I Believe and Up On the Roof?

6. Nurse Gladys Emmanuel was a regular character in which seventies TV show?

7. Janine Melnitz was the secretary for which group of supernatural heroes?

8. Whole Again was a hit for which girl group in 2000?

9. What was the name of the crime serial drama that launched in 2013 starring David Tennant?

10. Complete the movie title: Who Framed...?

ROUND 2: SCIENCE AND NATURE

1. A barometer is used to measure what?

2. Which H is one of the 4 basic chemical elements?

3. The scapula is the other name for which bone?

4. Which direction do birds fly in the winter?

5. Graphite is commonly found in which writing implement?

6. Rickets is caused by a lack of which vitamin?

7. In which region will you find the Barbary Macaques?

8. Mercury and Venus don't have what compared to the other planets?

9. What is a female alligator called?

10. How many toes does a cat have?

ROUND 3: FOOD AND DRINK

1. Barossa Valley wine region is in which country?

2. Necarines and peaches are almost genetically identical - true or false?

3. What is the alcohol base for a Moscow mule?

4. What is the correct name for egg white?

5. Cling film is known by which name in the USA?

6. What type of mint is Kendall mint cake flavoured with?

7. The sandwich was named after a real person-true or false?

8. How many segments are there inside an orange?

9. Sauerkraut is a German dish made up of chopped what?

10. What is an individual part of garlic called?

ROUND 4: SPORT

1. Who is the youngest ever winner of a F1 race?

2. In mile, how long is a marathon?

3. The Stanley cup is played for in which sport?

4. Who was the first professional footballer to be knighted?

5. Sebastian Coe won gold in which distance at the Olympics?

6. SW19 is the postcode for which tennis tournament?

7. A downhill ski trail is known by what name?

8. Allison Fisher is a famous name in which sport?

9. What does a red flag in motorsport signify?

10. A chukka is a period of play in which sport?

ROUND 5: GEBERAL KNOWLEDGE

1. The two major parties in US politics are Democrat and which other?

2. In the Bible, which book comes before Psalms?

3. When conferring a knighthood, which shoulder does the monarch touch first?

4. A lion holding a sword is on which country's flag?

5. What gas would you find in a lighter?

6. How many X chromosomes do women usually have?

7. The equinox means a day will consist of how many hours of daylight?

8. Which motorway links London and Swansea?

9. Natasha Romanoff is the alter ego of which superhero?

10. In Cluedo, the secret Passageway from the kitchen leads to which other room?

ANAGRAM

Name the British band from the anagram:
SLICE GRIPS

LINKS

What links the following:
Carrie, Charlotte, Samantha, Miranda

CRYPTIC CLUE

Name the 1937 book (and film trilogy of the same name) from the cryptic clue:
The stove part

Did You Know?

The scientific name for the fear of long words is hippopotomonstroses-quippedaliophobia.

Quiz 5

ROUND 1: ENTERTAINMENT

1. Who liked us Just the Way You Are in 2010?

2. Launched in 1990, complete the name of the topical panel show: Have I Got what?

3. Iron Man was the first movie in which comic book series of films?

4. True or false, the boy band A1 were from Norway as well as Britain?

5. Who was the first host of Big Brother UK?

6. The first rule of which movie is to not talk about it?

7. Who teamed up with Ed Sheeran on the 2019 hit I Don't Care?

8. John Thaw and Dennis Waterman starred in which seventies police drama?

9. Where was Clint Eastwood trying to escape from in 1979?

10. Ellie Goulding had a 2015 hit with Love Me Like what?

ROUND 2: SCIENCE AND NATURE

1. He is the chemical symbol for which element?

2. How long does it take the earth to complete one full turn on its axis?

3. What was Jake Garn the first person in space from what profession?

4. What part of the body would a podiatrist work on?

5. What is the part of a flower that becomes a fruit?

6. What is a squirrel's nest called?

7. Zoophobia is the fear of what?

8. Do eagles eat plants or meat?

9. What is the smallest breed of dog?

10. What is a male swan called?

ROUND 3: FOOD AND DRINK

1. Is a pumpkin a vegetable?

2. Port originates in which country?

3. Thin strips of vegetables are known as what kind of cut beginning with J?

4. Rolled oats, together with dried fruit, nuts and seeds are the main ingredients of which breakfast dish?

5. What do the Swedish call dishes served hot and cold as a buffet?

6. A magnum of champagne is made up of how many bottles?

7. Souffle is a baked dish of what?

8. What is the alcohol base for a cosmopolitan?

9. Clarified butter is called what in Asian cooking?

10. White chocolate is true chocolate, as it is made with pure cocoa beans-true or false?

ROUND 4: SPORT

1. Gary Lineker and Harry Kane are the only English players to win what?

2. Which stake do you start from traditionally at in the game of croquet?

3. The Ryder cup in golf is played between the USA and which other participant?

4. Which sport is played on the largest pitch?

5. Complete the NFL team name: Green Bay...?

6. Hop, skip and jump is associated with which sport?

7. The Americas Cup is a contest in which sport?

8. Who is the oldest person to win the Olympic 100 metre gold medal?

9. The mark on the floor that darts players must stand behind is called what?

10. Which venue is commonly referred to as the home of cricket?

ROUND 5: GEBERAL KNOWLEDGE

1. What is the name of Postman Pat's village?

2. Which month comes last alphabetically?

3. Who was the first British monarch of the 20th century?

4. What number do the two numbers on opposite sides of a dice always add up to?

5. In which UK cathedral is the Whispering Gallery?

6. What is the tower of a mosque called?

7. How many books make up the Bible's Old Testament?

8. Which car manufacturer makes the Jazz model?

9.   What does the B stand for in FBI?

10. Which metal is the best conductor of electricity?

ANAGRAM

Name the British football
team from the anagram:
ELECTRIC YETIS

LINKS

What links the following:
**Luke, Mark, John,
Matthew**

CRYPTIC CLUE

Name the former US
president from the
cryptic clue:
Wealthy solid steals boy

Did You Know?

The founder of
Pringles asked for his
ashes to be buried in
a Pringles can when
he died. His children
carried out his request.

Quiz 6

ROUND 1: ENTERTAINMENT

1. Boom Shake the Room was a 1993 hit for which duo?

2. Hannibal, Faceman, Murdock and BA Baracus were characters in which TV series?

3. Do You Want to Build a Snowman, and For the First Time in Forever were songs in which Disney musical?

4. What were One Republic counting in 2013 according to the song?

5. Which long-running police drama series came to an end in 2010?

6. Who played Indiana Jones throughout the movie series?

7. Jim Croce sang about Bad Bad who in 1973?

8. Polly Sherman was the waitress at which fictional hotel?

9. Complete the movie title: Four Weddings and a...?

10. Chico Slimani became famous on which TV talent show?

ROUND 2: SCIENCE AND NATURE

1. Which N is one of the four chemical elements?

2. Scurvy is a deficiency of which vitamin?

3. What do butterflies use to taste things?

4. An invertebrate doesn't have what?

5. Whales' blowholes help them do what?

6. What fuel would you need for a Bunsen burner?

7. What type of animal is a kookaburra?

8. Semolina is made from which grain?

9. Which animal has the longest gestation period?

10. Saffron comes from which flower?

ROUND 3: FOOD AND DRINK

1. The purple one, caramel swirl and the green triangle can be found in which chocolate tin?

2. What type of meat do the French call Canard?

3. What is the common British name for Bordeaux wine?

4. Foster's lager originates from which country?

5. Paella originates from which country?

6. Shortcrust, flaky and puff are all types of what?

7. What is the name for food on a skewer?

8. What is the alcohol base for a sidecar?

9. True or false, bananas are berries?

10. Arachibutyrophobia is a fear of which food getting stuck to the roof of your mouth?

ROUND 4: SPORT

1. Which English club has won the Champions League 6 times?

2. London and Sydney both have a cricket ground called what?

3. London and which other city have hosted the Olympic games 3 times?

4. What number comes between 5 and 1 on a darts board?

5. In amateur boxing, how many rounds make up a match?

6. Eldrick is the first name of which golfer?

7. What colour is the 8 ball in pool?

8. Drag racing is competed over what distance?

9. In rugby league, a drop goal is worth how many points?

10. In which sport do you throw stones at houses?

ROUND 5: GEBERAL KNOWLEDGE

1. What became the tallest building in the world when it opened in 1931?

2. What does the E represent In $E = Mc^2$?

3. Who created the character Noddy?

4. In which city was the Titanic constructed?

5. Margaret Thatcher resigned as leader of the Conservative party in which year?

6. In which newspaper did the first ever crossword appear?

7. The Post Office Tower changed its name to what in 1981?

8. Who is Barbie's male friend?

9. Betamax was the rival to which video format?

10. Theophobia Is A Fear Of what?

ANAGRAM

Name the type of bird
from the anagram:
SOLAR BATS

CRYPTIC CLUE

Name the comedian and
actress from the cryptic clue:
Triumph, a forest

LINKS

What links the following:
**Washington, Jefferson,
Roosevelt, Lincoln**

Did You Know?

Spiders' webs were used
as bandages in ancient
Greece and Rome.

Quiz 7

ROUND 1: ENTERTAINMENT

1. Who had a 1995 hit with Mysterious Girl?

2. Felicity Kendal, Richard Briers and Penelope Keith starred in which seventies sitcom?

3. Dougray Scott, Richard Roxburgh and Henry Cavill have all played villains in which movie franchise?

4. What nationality is Billie Eilish?

5. Which long-running TV talent show launched in 2007?

6. Once in a While and Time Warp are songs in which musical?

7. Stereophonics sang about Handbags and what in 2001?

8. Young Sheldon was a spin-off from which TV series?

9. With an all-star cast, what was the name of the film in which a group robbed 3 Las Vegas casinos?

10. Too Shy was a 1983 hit for which group?

ROUND 2: SCIENCE AND NATURE

1. What is the scientific name for the tonsils?

2. Which animal has the largest eyes?

3. Deciduous trees shed what every year?

4. What gender are the worker honeybees?

5. What speciality is a paediatric doctor?

6. Lions and hyenas share the same name for their home, which is called a what?

7. Force is equal to what times acceleration?

8. What is the opposite of nocturnal?

9. Do sharks blink?

10. Gingivitis is the inflammation of which part of the body?

ROUND 3: FOOD AND DRINK

1. What is the alcohol base for a Sex on the Beach?

2. What is the most expensive spice in the world?

3. Marrowfat is what kind of vegetable?

4. What is the main ingredient of an arctic roll?

5. Which word literally means twice cooked?

6. Venison comes from which animal?

7. A beef wellington is wrapped up in what?

8. Pancetta comes from which animal?

9. Often seen on a bottle of brandy, what does the s stand for in VSOP?

10. Tandoori dishes are cooked in what type of oven?

ROUND 4: SPORT

1. Which stadium is the home of the Football Association?

2. In golf, an eagle is how many under par?

3. Who was England captain when they regained the Ashes in 2005 after 18 years?

4. The art or love of toxophily is related to which sport?

5. The Rhinos are a rugby league team from which city?

6. In which sport would you need to use a map and compass?

7. Complete the NFL Team name: Miami...?

8. Which F1 constructor has won the most races?

9. How many points is the red ball worth in snooker?

10. How many players on a basketball team are allowed on the court at any time?

ROUND 5: GEBERAL KNOWLEDGE

1. Which fireman lives in Pontypandy?

2. Vera Lynn was known as the Forces' what?

3. Who was known as the "Voice of the Balls"?

4. Winnie the Pooh was owned by which boy?

5. The sea goat is the symbol of which zodiac sign?

6. Who painted the Sistine Chapel?

7. In which UK country would you find the town of Bethlehem?

8. Who was the roman god of the sea?

9. Which wife outlived Henry the Eighth?

10. What does the A stand for in FAQ?

ANAGRAM

Name the British author
from the anagram:
BIN REMOTELY

LINKS

What links the following:
**Leonardo, Raphael,
Donatello, Michelangelo**

CRYPTIC CLUE

Name the celebrity chef
from the cryptic clue:
Cheerful fruit

Did You Know?

A group of owls is
called a 'parliament'.

Quiz 8

ROUND 1: ENTERTAINMENT

1. Don't You Worry Child was a 2012 hit for which dance group?

2. What did the I stand for in KITT, the car from Knight Rider?

3. In which film did a group of oil drillers save the world from an asteroid?

4. Who sang about Sk8er Boi in 2002?

5. Lennie Godber, Norman Fletcher and Blanco Webb were prisoners in which TV show?

6. Because We Can, Come What May and Children of the Revolution were songs in which musical?

7. Come on You Reds was a UK number 1 for which football team in 1994?

8. According to the TV show title, Everybody Loves who...?

9. The Housemans visited the Catskill holiday resort in which Movie?

10. What was Bonnie Tyler holding out for in 1985?

ROUND 2: SCIENCE AND NATURE

1. The spleen destroys which colour blood cells?

2. How many pairs of ribs does an adult human have?

3. Galileo was the first person to see the moons of which planet?

4. What is the national flower of Holland?

5. What is a group of lions called?

6. How many eyes does a honey bee have?

7. What is a group of racoons known by?

8. In medical terms, what does the V stand for in DVT?

9. The emu is native to which country?

10. Can seeds grow in water without soil?

ROUND 3: FOOD AND DRINK

1. Grolsch originates from which country?

2. What is the vitamin found in carrots?

3. How many base liquors are there?

4. Ice cream covered with a meringue and then baked in an oven is called a what?

5. Fish and seafood provide omega what?

6. Spaghetti traditionally has which cheese sprinkled on top of it?

7. A frappe is made using thinly crushed what?

8. Which spice comes from the inner part of a tree?

9. Lachanophobia is the fear of which food type?

10. What ingredient causes bread to rise?

ROUND 4: SPORT

1. In football, who plays their home games at Stamford Bridge?

2. How many F1 world titles did Stirling Moss win?

3. Chester-Le-Street cricket ground is in which county?

4. The Wire is the nickname for which rugby league club?

5. What is the name of a person who carries a golfer's bag?

6. Keirin is a discipline in which sport?

7. What is the oldest belt in British boxing called?

8. How many players are there in a baseball team?

9. How wide in inches is the Beam in women's Gymnastics?

10. Complete the NFL team name: Denver?

ROUND 5: GEBERAL KNOWLEDGE

1. Hypertension is the medical name for what condition?

2. What does F stand for in FM Radio?

3. What is the first letter of the Greek alphabet?

4. Allegro in music is likely to be played how?

5. Crystal is the traditional anniversary gift for which year?

6. Charles Schulz created which comic strip?

7. The Millennium Stadium is in which UK city?

8. D represents what number in Roman numerals?

9. What is the medical name for short-sightedness?

10. Statler and Waldorf were puppets in which TV series?

ANAGRAM

Name the American former
Wimbledon champion from
the anagram:
RICHER VETS

CRYPTIC CLUE

Name the UK city
from the cryptic clue:
Goose ocean

LINKS

What links the following:
**Kings Cross, Fenchurch
Street, Liverpool Street,
Marylebone**

Did You Know?

The original name
of search engine
Google was Backrub.

Quiz 9

WORLD RECORD QUIZ

This was the quiz from the world record breaking night. 182,513 people tuned in to the live stream and broke the world record most viewers of a quiz live stream (YouTube).

ROUND 1: TV AND FILM

1. Which TV show's theme tune asks if Mr Hitler is kidding?

2. What was the name of the café owner in Allo Allo?

3. The Big Breakfast launched in 1992 with Gaby Roslin and which other host?

4. What was the name of the MI5 BBC drama that launched in 2002 and ran for 10 series?

5. Who wrote the first series of Killing Eve?

6. Matt Damon was left for dead on Mars in which movie?

7. Jamie Bell played the lead role in which British 2000s dance film?

8. Released in 1995, what was the name of the first completely computer-animated feature film?

9. What was the name of the tower in Die Hard?

10. Liza Minelli starred in which 1972 musical, set in 1930s Berlin?

ROUND 2: SPORTS AND LEISURE

1. Who scored England's last-gasp winning drop goal in the 2003 RugbyWorld Cup Final against Australia?

2. The Olympics have been re-arranged to from 2020 to 2021 but what month will they start? May, June or July?

3. Who has won the most majors in Golf? Tiger Woods or Jack Nicholson?

4. How many players are there on a standard volleyball team?

5. The Boat Race takes place between which two universities?

6. Which board game has a cheater and an ultimate banking edition?

7. Becoming is a 2018 book written by whom?

8. Defying Gravity is a song from which musical?

9. Which UK city is the home of the National Rail Museum?

10. In which board game would you find Miss Scarlet and Professor Plum?

ROUND 3: MUSIC

1. Which boyband returned after a 10-year hiatus in 2019 with their hit Hello My Love?

2. What is Stormzy's real first name?

3. Who said we could stand under her Umbrella in 2007?

4. According to the title of the song, who did Katy Perry Kiss in 2008?

5. Who is Reginald Dwight better known as?

6. In which Oasis song did he not get on with her brother, bad had a thing for her mother?

7. Whitney Houston wanted to dance with who in the eighties?

8. What's Love Got To Do With It, was an eighties hit for who?

9. Stairway to Heaven was a 1971 hit for who?

10. In which Queen hit could they barely stand on their feet, looked in the mirror and cried?

ROUND 4: FOOD AND DRINK

1. In the USA it is known as an eggplant, but what is it called in the UK?

2. En croute means what in French?

3. Which sweet wanted us to Taste the Rainbow?

4. Which UK beer has a blue 5-pointed star on its label?

5. What is the main seasoning of goulash?

6. What is the world's most manufactured drink?

7. What are the three main ingredients you would need to make a mocha?

8. How would you make the drink snakebite?

9. What is unusual about a Lorne sausage in Scotland?

10. What does gin get its predominant flavour from?

ROUND 5: GEBERAL KNOWLEDGE

1. What is the highest number used in standard sudoku?

2. Where in the world would you expect to find a car with the vehicle registration code V?

3. The logo for which popular app consists of a white telephone in a white speech bubble on a green background?

4. What was the name of the 4th book in the Harry Potter Series?

5. Moonshine was a slang term for what kind of beverage?

6. Who was the last UK act to win Eurovision?

7. True or false, the Bahamas is made up of 700 individual islands?

8. The World Health Organization is based in which city?

9. Blue Moon, Hopelessly Devoted to You and Summer Nights are songs from which musical?

10. In the Bible, who built the Ark?

ANAGRAM

Name the former UK prime minister from the anagram:

SHAM EATERY

CRYPTIC CLUE

Name the British TV personality from the cryptic clue:

Naked barbecues

LINKS

What links the following:

Stag, Ground, Dung, Leaf

Did You Know?

On 18 April 1930, the BBC reported that there was 'no news today' and played piano music for 15 minutes in place of the 20:45 news bulletin.

Quiz 10

ROUND 1: ENTERTAINMENT

1. What was the final song from One Direction before they split up?

2. Will Smith was the Fresh Prince of where?

3. Hugh Jackman starred in which 2017 musical?

4. That's Not My Name was a 2008 hit for which group?

5. Gunther ran the coffee shop in which tv show?

6. Who played James Bond in On Her Majesty's Secret Service?

7. Papa Don't Preach, Like a Prayer and La Isla Bonita were eighties hits for which female artist?

8. Tobey Maguire, Andrew Garfield and Tom Holland have all played which superhero?

9. Snap sang that rhythm is a what in 1992?

10. Whoopi Goldberg went into witness protection as a nun in which film?

ROUND 2: SCIENCE AND NATURE

1. The radius is a bone in which part of the body?

2. What was the name of the first dog in space?

3. Cork comes from which part of a tree?

4. Nimbus clouds produce what?

5. The aorta carries what away from the heart?

6. Li is the chemical symbol for which element?

7. What is missing from a Manx cat compared to others?

8. Worker ants are female - true or false?

9. What would you count to tell the age of a tree?

10. The lumbar is what part of the body?

ROUND 3: FOOD AND DRINK

1. Prunes come from which dried fruit?

2. A kipper is a smoked what?

3. What is the alcohol base for a pina colada?

4. Profiteroles use what type of pastry?

5. Which other fruit can you make from the letters in the word Lemon?

6. What food is permitted to be eaten under Jewish dietary laws?

7. Which country do enchiladas originate from?

8. What was the former name of Starburst?

9. True or false: avocados are a vegetable?

10. According to the secret recipe, how many herbs and spices are there in KFC chicken?

ROUND 4: SPORTS

1. At the end of the 2019/20 season, who had won the most Premier League titles?

2. Edgbaston cricket ground is in which city?

3. In the decathlon, what is the last event?

4. What is the female version of the Ryder Cup called?

5. A rugby union match lasts how many minutes?

6. Who holds the record for the most pole positions in F1?

7. Which golfer was nicknamed the Golden Bear?

8. The Wallabies is the nickname of which rugby union country?

9. How old was Martina Hingis when she first won a Wimbledon singles title?

10. How many colours make up the Olympic rings?

ROUND 5: GEBERAL KNOWLEDGE

1. The Kalahari desert is on which continent?

2. RSM is the vehicle registration code for which country?

3. An MEP is a member of which parliament?

4. Paul Hewson is the real name of which singer?

5. What colour are trams on the London Underground map?

6. Fort William is the nearest town to which mountain?

7. The Balearic Islands are in which body of water?

8. Sternutation is the act of what?

9. Martin Luther King was assassinated in which year?

10. What is the currency of Malaysia?

ANAGRAM

Name the hit US TV
show from the anagram:
BANK BRIGADE

CRYPTIC CLUE

Name the European capital
city from the cryptic clue:
Goods house

LINKS

What links the following:
**Eric, Stanley, Kyle,
Kenny**

Did You Know?

Queen Elizabeth II is
a trained mechanic.

Quiz 11

ROUND 1: ENTERTAINMENT

1. Someone You Loved was a 2019 hit for which artist?

2. David Mitchell and Robert Webb starred together in which Channel 4 comedy series?

3. Vanellope von Schweetz and Fix-It Felix were characters in which movie?

4. Move, Power and Touch were hits for which girl band?

5. Which Doctor Who spin-off ended in 2011?

6. Complete the 1974 movie title: The Towering...?

7. Finish the Abba song title, Knowing Me...?

8. Hunted was a reality TV series launched on which channel?

9. Who directed Jaws?

10. Bob Marley and Eric Clapton both sang about shooting who in the seventies?

ROUND 2: SCIENCE AND NATURE

1. Ag is the chemical symbol for which element?

2. What would you use a Geiger counter for?

3. In medical terms, what does the A stand for in ADHD?

4. The trachea is the medical name for what in the body?

5. Nosocomephobia is the fear of what?

6. Which animal usually lays the biggest egg?

7. Which is the only bird that can fly backwards?

8. How can you tell a male and female lion apart by looking at them?

9. Which bird has the longest wingspan?

10. The mosquito can infect humans with which disease?

ROUND 3: FOOD AND DRINK

1. What is the name for a wine that has been heated and had spices added to it?

2. John Pemberton invented which fizzy drink in 1886?

3. Rotelle is what shape of pasta?

4. Carlsberg originates from which country?

5. Sugar and beaten egg whites make up which dessert?

6. What was the former name of the chocolate bar Snickers?

7. The alcoholic drink Perry is distilled from which fruit?

8. Batter and what ingredient make up toad in the hole?

9. Calamari is the Italian name for which fish food?

10. Caviar comes from which fish?

ROUND 4: SPORT

1. At the end of the 2019/20 season, who was the Premier League's record top goalscorer?

2. What does the B stand for in LBW?

3. At the 1936 Olympics, how many medals did Jesse Owens win?

4. What was the first English football club to be floated on a stock exchange in 1983?

5. Which sporting event starts at Putney and ends at Mortlake?

6. Torvill and Dean were famous in which sport?

7. Ice Hockey originates from which country?

8. How many extra runs are awarded for a no ball?

9. With which club would you associate the name Galacticos?

10. The winners of which tournament were originally awarded the Jules Rimet Trophy?

ROUND 5: GEBERAL KNOWLEDGE

1. If you cross the International Date Line from the west, do you lose a day or gain one?

2. XIX is what number in roman numerals?

3. GBG is the vehicle registration code for which island?

4. Who was the first wife of Henry the Eighth

5. Jenny Jerome was the mother of which famous politician?

6. Gatso is the alternate name for which roadside device?

7. How did Al Capone die?

8. Aphrodite is the Greek goddess of what?

9. Dr Seuss wrote about the Cat in the what?

10. Traitor's Gate in between the Tower of London and what?

ANAGRAM

Name the UK national park from the anagram:
TRACKSIDE TIP

LINKS

What links the following:
Chico, Harpo, Groucho, Zeppo

CRYPTIC CLUE

Name the musical instrument from the cryptic clue:
Cylindrical pub

Did You Know?

If all the arteries and veins in one human body were laid out end to end, their total length could encircle the earth nearly two and a half times.

Quiz 12

ROUND 1: ENTERTAINMENT

1. Relax and Two Tribes were hit for which group?

2. Will, Simon, Jay and Neil were the lead characters in which TV show and films?

3. What was the sequel to Jurassic Park?

4. Eye of the Tiger was a 1982 hit for which group?

5. "Gotta catch em all!" What was the name of the children's TV show?

6. Complete the 1979 movie title: Kramer vs...?

7. Maggie May was a 1971 hit for whom?

8. Richard O'Brien was the first host of which game show?

9. What number was always on Herbie in the film series?

10. Who was Livin' La Vida Loca in 1999?

ROUND 2: SCIENCE AND NATURE

1. Which is the world's largest ocean?

2. A conker comes from which tree?

3. Which scientist devised the three laws of motion?

4. Jupiter, Neptune, Saturn and Uranus are known as the what giants?

5. Where in the body might you suffer from Carpal Tunnel?

6. What is the vitamin that helps to clot blood?

7. Which bird was taken down to mines to detect dangerous gases?

8. How many stomachs does a cow have?

9. Which body part is used to measure horses?

10. What is a male pig called?

ROUND 3: FOOD AND DRINK

1. A rose wine is what colour?

2. What meat is traditionally used in Moussaka?

3. Sweetcorn is a type of which cereal grain?

4. Which foil colour top indicates
   whole milk in traditional glass milk bottles?

5. Sloe is the fruit of which tree?

6. What does the I stand for in IPA?

7. Ratatouille is a French dish made up what kind
   of stew?

8. Basmati is a type of what?

9. What kind of pasta is ravioli?

10. On a bottle of wine, what is the punt?

ROUND 4: GEOGRAPHY

1. Kabul is the capital city of which country?

2. Which is the UK's longest suspension bridge?

3. Which river flows through Paris?

4. Which is the smallest of all the continents?

5. The city of New York is on which river?

6. Rapa Nui is the native name for which island?

7. Schiphol airport serves which city?

8. In which city would you find the Red Square?

9. In which US state can you find the Liberty Bell and Gettysburg?

10. What is the largest park in Greater London?

ROUND 5: GEBERAL KNOWLEDGE

1. Runnymede saw the signing of which document in 1215?

2. The Ashes in cricket are played between England and which other nation?

3. A firkin contains how many gallons?

4. What is the name of an edible fungus that grows underground?

5. What is the main ingredient of black pudding?

6. In which London street would you find the Cenotaph?

7. Which date is St David's Day?

8. In 1963, Aboriginals were allowed to vote for the first time in which country?

9. What is the name of Harry Potter's school?

10. Glaucoma affects which part of the body?

ANAGRAM

Name the London tube
station from the anagram:
INKSTONE SHOTGUN

LINKS

What links the following:
**French, German, Italian,
Romansh**

CRYPTIC CLUE

Name the film from the
cryptic clue:
Tumble from heaven

Did You Know?

Salvador Dalí
designed the wrapper
for Chupa Chups.

9. Which has the largest wingspan of any living bird?

10. Which element has the atomic number 1?

ROUND 2: TV AND FILM

1. How many contestants are on each team in University Challenge?

2. Who played Phileas Fogg in the 2004 film comedy version of Around the World in 80 Days?

3. Who played Rachel Green in the TV series Friends?

4. Which game show has been presented by the following presenters: Richard O'Brien, Ed Tudor Pole, Stephen Merchant and Richard Ayoade?

5. Men in Brown is a mini series and sketch on which entertainment duo's current TV show?

6. Who narrates Love Island?

7. What was the name of Harry Potter's owl?

8. Who won Britain's Got Talent in June 2018?

9. What was the name of the character played by Sean Bean in Game of Thrones?

10. Who played Doc Emmett Brown in the Back to the Future series?

Quiz 13

ROUND 1: ENTERTAINMENT

1. Camila Cabello was a singer with which girl band?

2. Richard Madden Played David Budd in which BBC drama?

3. What is the name of the song that Ferris Bueller sings in the film named after him?

4. Tracey Chapman sang about a fast what in 1988?

5. Which long running children's television drama finally ended in 2008 after 30 years on screen?

6. What did Kevin and Perry go according to the movie title?

7. I Gotta Feeling, Boom Boom Pow and My Humps were hits for which American group?

8. What was the name of the female smurf?

9. Leonardo DiCaprio played Jack Dawson in which movie?

10. Who sang with Bradley Cooper on the 2018 song Shallow?

ROUND 2: SCIENCE AND NATURE

1. Cl is the chemical symbol for which chemical element?

2. The tibia is known by which other name?

3. The National Trust has what tree's leaves as its symbol?

4. What is the scientific name for alcohol?

5. What is a female donkey called?

6. What is the collective name for a group of rhinoceros?

7. Mosquitos have teeth - true or false?

8. What is a baby lion called?

9. What is a group of crows called?

10. What is the tallest grass in the world?

ROUND 3: FOOD AND DRINK

1. The annatto seed has been used to colour which kind of cheese?

2. The word demi-sec on a bottle of champagne indicates it is what?

3. What is the main base for Bouillabaisse?

4. What herb is found in pesto sauce?

5. Rigatoni is what shape of pasta?

6. What is used to flavour Pernod?

7. The river Spey supplies water for 90% of which alcohol?

8. Chop Suey originated in which country?

9. What milk type is the basic ingredient in Thai cooking?

10. What is the alcohol base for a mojito?

ROUND 4: WHO SAID IT?

1. The greatest glory in living lies not in never falling, but in rising every time we fall?

2. Spread love everywhere you go. Let no one ever come to you without leaving happier?

3. Whoever is happy will make others happy too?

4. We are not makers of history. We are made by history?

5. History is the version of past events that people have decided to agree upon?

6. It is better to offer no excuse than a bad one?

7. A man is not finished when he is defeated. He is finished when he quits?

8. No great discovery was ever made without a bold guess?

9. Knowing yourself is the beginning of all wisdom?

10. That's one small step for man, one giant leap for mankind?

ROUND 5: GEBERAL KNOWLEDGE

1. Lisbon is the capital of which country?

2. What day does a month need to start on, for it to have a Friday the 13th?

3. A 14-line poem is known as a what?

4. A butterfly has how many wings?

5. Lyndon B Johnson is a former president of which country?

6. Tom Hanks played which character in The Da Vinci Code?

7. Who is on the back of the current £5 note?

8. On which island would you find Paphos?

9. What does the F stand for in UFO?

10. XV is what in Roman numerals number?

ANAGRAM

Name the car manufacturer from the anagram:

BOILING HARM

CRYPTIC CLUE

Name the song from the cryptic clue:

Slim monarch speaking audibly

LINKS

What links the following:

James Vaughan, James Milner, Wayne Rooney, Cesc Fabregas

Did You Know?

The last time Liechtenstein fought in a war was in 1866. None of their 80 soldiers were injured, and they returned with an extra man – a new Italian "friend" they had picked up on the way.

Quiz 14

ROUND 1: ENTERTAINMENT

1. Who was All About That Bass in 2014?

2. Russell Tovey starred as a werewolf in which BBC 3 supernatural comedy?

3. Complete the book and movie title: Harry Potter and The Prisoner of...?

4. Finish the title of the Mika song: Grace...?

5. Who was the alter ego of the Bionic Woman?

6. Dave Franco, Jesie Eisenberg, Woody Harrelson and Isla Fisher starred as magicians in which film?

7. Dreadlock Holiday was a 1978 hit for which group?

8. It's a Hard Knock Life, Let's Go to the Movies and Tomorrow are songs from which musical?

9. What was the name of the seventies TV show set in Edwardian London based around the Bellamy family?

10. How many things did they hate about you according to the movie title?

ROUND 2: SCIENCE AND NATURE

1. Ne is the chemical symbol for which element?

2. Dermatology is associated with which part of the body?

3. Cashmere comes from which animal?

4. Which bird can swim the fastest?

5. What is a male rabbit called?

6. Amphibian is a term used for an animal that can live on land and what?

7. Spider, Ghost, and Shore are all types of what?

8. What is a group of monkeys called?

9. True or false, the fluid of tiger moths is posionous?

10. The Patella is the scientific name for which body part?

ROUND 3: FOOD AND DRINK

1. Burgundy is a wine region in which country?

2. The liqueur Kahlua has which flavour?

3. Sparkling wine and stout beer make up which cocktail?

4. What is the key ingredient of a Rosti?

5. What does ABV stand for?

6. Buffalo milk is turned into which cheese?

7. On average what has more vitamin C, oranges or red peppers?

8. Mageirocophobia is the fear of what?

9. Cointreau has what flavour as its base?

10. Pule cheese is made from the milk of which animal?

ROUND 4: ART & LITERATURE

1. Miss Marple was created by which author?

2. Which author has the pen name, Richard Bachman?

3. Which city is home to the Muse Picasso?

4. What was the name of the hedgehog in the Beatrix Potter tales?

5. What was found at the back of the wardrobe in novels by CS Lewis?

6. Michael Flatley became famous with which dance troupe?

7. TS Eliot said which month is the cruellest?

8. The Mona Lisa is in which museum?

9. Pop Art was introduced by which painter?

10. David Hockney frequently uses what water feature in his paintings?

ROUND 5: GEBERAL KNOWLEDGE

1. Which C is one of the four basic chemical elements?

2. DXB is the international code for which airport?

3. MMMM is what number in roman numerals?

4. Because You're Worth It is the slogan for which company?

5. Bogota is the capital city of which country?

6. Which US state was the TV series Dallas set?

7. Are you allowed to play left-handed in Polo?

8. In which ocean would you find the Canary Islands?

9. What was the crime that Anne Boleyn was convicted of?

10. What does the G stand for in GP?

ANAGRAM

Name the cocktail from
the anagram:
COPILOTS MOAN

CRYPTIC CLUE

Name the flower from
the cryptic clue:
Automobile country

LINKS

What links the following:
**Elizabeth, George,
Edward, George**

Did You Know?

The US Supreme
Court has its own
private basketball court
nicknamed "the highest
court in the land".

Quiz 15

ROUND 1: SCIENCE AND NATURE

1. What is the name for a female horse under the age of four?

2. What is a baby deer called?

3. What is a fear of spiders called?

4. Which O is one of the four basic chemical elements?

5. Ornithology is the study of what?

6. Where in the body night you find the jugular vein?

7. Whales' blowholes help them do what?

8. How many toes does a camel have?

9. K is the chemical symbol for which chemical element?

10. In which year did the Icelandic ash cause widespread travel disruptions?

ROUND 2: FOOD AND DRINK

1. Where do cranberries grow?

2. Aosta Valley is a wine region in which country?

3. What is bruschetta?

4. How many normal-size bottles does a Jeroboam hold?

5. What is the UK's best-selling soup flavour?

6. What is the alcohol base for a margarita?

7. What sauce is traditionally served with pork?

8. What is tofu made of?

9. The Jack Daniel's Distillery is located in which state?

10. What is another name for gelato?

ROUND 3: GEOGRAPHY

1. The backs are the canals in which UK city?

2. In which year did the Channel Tunnel see public train services start running?

3. Dhaka is the capital of which country?

4. Fort Worth airport is in which US state?

5. The Herald of Free Enterprise capsized when leaving which port?

6. What is the longest river in the UK?

7. Bolivia and Paraguay don't have a coastline - true or false?

8. In which ocean would you find Mauritius?

9. What is the world's longest mountain range?

10. Transylvania is in which modern day country?

ROUND 4: MOVIE TAGLINES

1. The last man on earth is not alone

2. The bride gets the thrills, the father gets the bills

3. One man's struggle to take it easy

4. Check in. Unpack. Relax. Take a shower.

5. In space no one can hear you scream

6. The longer you wait, the harder it gets

7. You don't get to 500 million friends without making a few enemies

8. You'll believe a man can fly

9. Escape or die frying

10. This is Benjamin. He's a little worried about his future

ROUND 5: GEBERAL KNOWLEDGE

1. Who was the assassination target in the novel The Day of the Jackal?

2. LXXXII what is the Roman numeral?

3. Just Do It is the slogan for which company?

4. Moses was talking to who in the burning bush?

5. What US charity is the equivalent of the Guide Dogs?

6. What year did Margaret Thatcher become prime minister?

7. Which country hosted the summer Olympic Games of 2000?

8. An individual judge can award what highest score in figure skating?

9. Arnold Schwarzenegger, Bruce Willis and Sylvester Stallone backed the foundation of which restaurant chain?

10. Super Mario can be found on which console series?

Quiz 15

ANAGRAM

Name the British TV presenter from the anagram:
SLAYED COYOTE

LINKS

What links the following:
Mick, Keith, Charlie, Ronnie

CRYPTIC CLUE

Name the children's character from the cryptic clue:
Brusque chap

Did You Know?

Otters hold hands while they sleep to stop them floating away from each other.

Quiz 16

ROUND 1: COMPANY SLOGANS

1. The best a man can get

2. Have it your way

3. The happiest place on earth

4. The ultimate driving machine

5. Good to the last drop

6. It's in the game

7. Snap! Crackle! Pop!

8. I'm lovin' it

9. Maybe she's born with it

10. The king of beers

ROUND 2: HISTORY

1. Which king was killed at the Battle of Hastings?

2. What was the other name for the Plague that arrived in England in the 1300s?

3. The War of the Roses took place between the House of York and which other house?

4. In which century was William Shakespeare born?

5. Who was Guy Fawkes trying to assassinate?

6. Who led the allies to victory at Waterloo?

7. Queen Victoria ascended the throne in which year?

8. What date is associated with VJ Day?

9. Prince Charles was invested as the Prince of Wales in which year?

10. In which year did Queen Elizabeth II celebrate her diamond jubilee?

ROUND 3: CAPITAL CITIES NAME THE COUNTRY

1. Havana

2. Kampala

3. Montevideo

4. New Delhi

5. Seoul

6. Tallinn

7. Caracas

8. Cairo

9. Bridgetown

10. Bratislava

ROUND 4: CHEMICAL SYMBOLS

1. Mg

2. Ar

3. Si

4. Ni

5. Cu

6. Zn

7. Pd

8. Xe

9. Hf

10. Hg

ROUND 5: GEBERAL KNOWLEDGE

1. Who was the Greek god of Love?

2. Making Your Mind Up was a hit for which group?

3. Monaco has the shortest European what?

4. Ginger, Posh, Scary, Sporty and Baby made up which girl group?

5. Who has played James Bond more times, Pierce Brosnan or Sean Connery?

6. Radio Caroline was considered to be what kind of broadcaster?

7. Colonel Sanders started which fast food chain?

8. Who entertained the nation with PE lessons during the UK lockdown in 2020?

9. What colour is the Northern Line on the London Underground map?

10. Houston Airport is named after which former president?

ANAGRAM

Name the kitchen
implement from
the anagram:
SHAMPOO TREAT

CRYPTIC CLUE

Name the comedian
from the cryptic clue:
Gallic daybreak

LINKS

What links the following:
**Dodgers, Lakers, Rams,
Galaxy**

Did You Know?

Cinema goers in
Colombia often snack
on roasted ants rather
than popcorn.

Quiz 17

VIRTUAL PUB QUIZ SATURDAY CHARITY SPECIAL

The first charity special and Live Saturday Quiz. The final round was questions asked by Celebrities and NHS Keyworkers. They set their own questions.

ROUND 1: ENTERTAINMENT

1. Robert Downey Junior plays the title role in which 2020 film?

2. Will Smith and Martin Lawrence reprised their roles for a third time in which 2020 movie?

3. Starring Al Pacino, Joe Pesci and Robert De Niro, which film was released exclusively on Netflix in 2019?

4. Maverick, Iceman and Goose were characters in which film?

5. Marlon Brando played which character in The Godfather?

6. Who played Jack Bauer's daughter in the TV series 24?

7. Steve Carrell plays a character loosely based on Ricky Gervais' character in which TV series?

8. Barney Stinson, Ted Mosby and Robin Scherbatsky were characters in which hit TV series?

9. "In 1972, a crack commando unit was sent to prison by a military court for a crime they didn't commit" is the start to which TV series?

10. Name the TV series based around the New Directions?

ROUND 2: SPORT AND LEISURE

1. Name the card game named after the Spanish name for one.

2. What do you need to play the game craps?

3. How many dominoes are there in a double six set?

4. How many different topics are there in a game of Trivial Pursuit?

5. What does scuba in scuba diving stand for?

6. Name the 4 English clubs that competed in the Champions League and Europa League Finals in 2019?

7. Complete the American Football Team Name, New York...?

8. What is considered the national sport of Japan?

9. Where in the UK does one of the Grand Slam tournaments in tennis takes place?

10. Who is the current England Women's Football Team Captain?

ROUND 3: MUSIC

1. Justin Timberlake was formerly in which band?

2. What is the name of the parody king with hits such as Another One Rides the Bus, Eat It and Amish Paradise?

3. Who left One Direction in 2015, breaking the hearts of millions of fans?

4. Who sang House of the Rising Sun in 1964?

5. In which song will the groove and the friends try to move your feet?

6. How many things is Rick Astley never going to do to you in Never Gonna Give You Up?

7. Isaac, Taylor and Zac made up which pop brothers?

8. What did MC Hammer say we couldn't touch?

9. According to the 1999 hit, who had a girl in Paris, Rome and even the Vatican Dome?

10. Who has the most UK number 1 singles according to the official charts?

ROUND 4: SCIENCE, NATURE AND TECHNOLOGY

1. What is the home of a badger called?

2. Cos is a type of what?

3. What is the largest key on a standard keyboard?

4. Which element has the chemical symbol U?

5. What was the name of the first cloned sheep?

6. When dipped in acid, what colour does litmus paper turn to?

7. What is measured in decibels?

8. How many colours are in the rainbow?

9. What social media platform did a viral video featuring Dame Judi Dench appear on?

10. What was the grape that Fred discovered and put into a wine in Gordon, Gino and Fred when they were in Mexico?

ROUND 5: GEBERAL KNOWLEDGE – NHS AND CELEBS

1. Which is the only city to have hosted the Olympics 3 times?

2. **Graham Cole from The Bill:** What was his character's badge number? And what was his favourite job in the police?

3. What is the longest and strongest bone in the body?

4. **James from The Vamps:** In the 2014 BBC Teen awards, how many awards did The Vamps win?

5. What is the largest organ OF the human body?

6. **Cathy Newman**: Which cabinet minister is related to a member of The Clash?

7. In what year was the NHS formed?

8. **Tyger Drew-Honey**: what was his first TV job?

9. Who scored the winning goal in the 2013 FA Cup Final as Wigan beat Man City?

10. **Will Poulter:**What is the name of the TLC song that featured in We're the Millers?

ANAGRAM

Name the river from
the anagram:
SUMO SIRI

CRYPTIC CLUE

Name the historical figure
from the cryptic clue:
**Gain rocky chapel
mound**

LINKS

What links the following:
**Common, Rock, Stock,
Turtle**

Did You Know?

At US President Andrew
Jackson's funeral in
1845, his pet parrot
started swearing loudly
and had to be removed.

Quiz 18

ROUND 1: ENTERTAINMENT

1. What was the spin-off from Life on Mars called?

2. Who replaced Nick Hewer on The Apprentice?

3. Who hosted Deal or No Deal?

4. Everybody's Free To Wear Sunscreen was a 1999 hit for whom?

5. Curtis Stigers had a 1992 hit with You're All That Matters to what?

6. Which song has spent longer at number 1 in the UK Charts: (Everything I Do) I Do It For You by Bryan Adams or Love Is All Around by Wet Wet Wet?

7. Luke Goss and Matt Goss were in which band?

8. "We are not alone" is the tagline to which movie?

9. Who starred as John Kimble, an undercover policeman working in a kindergarten?

10. Maverick, Goose, and Ice Man are characters in which movie?

ROUND 2: SCIENCE AND NATURE

1. What d bees use as thier source of energy?

2. What does USB stand for?

3. Of the 118 elements in the periodic table how many are naturally occurring: 34, 64 or 94?

4. Which organ produces insulin?

5. Which animal lives in a coop?

6. Na is the chemical symbol for what?

7. Sciatic is the largest what in the human body?

8. Botany is the study of what?

9. Which chemical element has the shortest name?

10. What is the liquid metal at the centre of the of the Moon?

ROUND 3: FOOD AND DRINK

1. What is a sorbet?

2. Orange juice and champagne makes which drink?

3. How many teaspoons are there in 10 tablespoons?

4. Which country would you get Rioja wine from?

5. Venison comes from which animal?

6. Crème de menthe is which colour drink?

7. A bloody Mary contains which alcoholic liquid?

8. Which vegetable is an emblem of Wales?

9. Prunes are dried what?

10. A margherita pizza consists of cheese and which other ingredient?

ROUND 4: SPORT

1. Name the football team nicknamed the Blades?

2. How many different scoring areas are there on a darts board?

3. In the Tour de France, what colour jersey does the leader wear?

4. Duckworth Lewis is a method used to decide the winner in which sport?

5. Which country has the oldest ever golf course?

6. Who was the first British club to win a European football trophy?

7. Which club has won the most Rugby Super League Grand Finals?

8. Sebastian Vettel made his F1 debut with which team?

9. Which county cricket club plays at Lord's?

10. At which racecourse would you watch the Grand National?

ROUND 5: GEBERAL KNOWLEDGE

1. Who was Barack Obama's Vice President?

2. What is the Roman numeral for 1000?

3. Which was the first British bank to use an ATM?

4. In which year was the British rail network nationalised?

5. In which nursery rhyme did the cow jump over the moon?

6. In which city is the UK's largest cathedral by area?

7. The World Wildlife Fund has which animal as its emblem?

8. Ant and Dec found fame on which children's TV series?

9. Complete this William Shakespeare play: The Merchant of…?

10. What is an autobahn in Germany?

ANAGRAM

Name the cartoon character from the anagram:
SNIFFLED ROTTEN

CRYPTIC CLUE

Name the flower from the cryptic clue:
Alternative child

LINKS

What links the following:
Alan Turing, Julian Assange, Hamlet, Dominic Cummings

Did You Know?

You are much more likely to be killed by a vending machine than you are to be killed by a shark.

Quiz 19

ROUND 1: MUSIC

1. Freddy Mercury was the lead singer with which band?

2. Maureen, Anne, Linda and Coleen made up which female group?

3. You'll Never Walk Alone was released by which group in 1963?

4. Who joined Kiki Dee on Don't Go Breaking My Heart?

5. Frankie Goes to Hollywood sang about two what in the eighties?

6. Tim Burgess is the lead singer of which British band?

7. All the Things She Said was a hit for whom?

8. Pompeii was a 2013 hit for whom?

9. Who won the reality TV series Popstars: the Rivals?

10. What song did Blue sing at Eurovision?

ROUND 2: HISTORY

1. Who did Mozambique declare independence from?

2. The Monument in London is a reminder of which event?

3. Who was James I's mother?

4. The charge of the light brigade featured in which battle?

5. Jamaica became independent from whom in 1962?

6. The first package holiday was arranged from Leicester to Loughborough by which man?

7. Louise Joy Brown was the world's first what?

8. What was the name of the first female British cabinet minister?

9. Which embassy did the SAS storm to end a siege in 1980?

10. In which country was Greenpeace founded?

ROUND 3: CHEMICAL SYMBOLS

1. P

2. Co

3. Mn

4. Ga

5. As

6. Zr

7. In

8. Sn

9. Ce

10. W

ROUND 4: COMPANY SLOGANS

1. Impossible is nothing

2. What's in your wallet?

3. It's the real thing

4. There are some things money can't buy

5. Have a break

6. Beanz meanz

7. It does exactly what it says on the tin

8. Vorsprung durch Technik

9. You either love it or hate it

10. Refreshes the parts other beers cannot reach

ROUND 5: GEBERAL KNOWLEDGE

1. Who is the Greek messenger of the gods?

2. What does the A stand for in SAS?

3. What is a produced in a ginnery?

4. In which country was Mel Gibson born?

5. Bibliophobia is a fear of what?

6. Which is the only piece able to jump over another piece at any time in a game of chess?

7. What is the birthstone for September?

8. Which American state ends with 3 vowels?

9. What is the last book of the New Testament?

10. The GoldenEye game was based around which secret service agent?

ANAGRAM

Name the UK magazine
from the anagram:
**ATONING
ARCHIPELAGO**

CRYPTIC CLUE

Name the car manufacturer
from the cryptic clue:
Tearful slander

LINKS

What links the following:
**California, Arizona, New
Mexico, Texas**

Did You Know?

Lobsters pee out
of their heads.

Quiz 20

ROUND 1: MOVIES

1. Who directed Avatar?

2. Who was the voice of Simba in the 2019 Lion King remake?

3. Who played Ron Weasley in the Harry Potter films?

4. Scarlet and Herb Overkill were the villains in which movie?

5. Who played Captain Marvel in the 2019 film?

6. Solo is a spin-off movie from which franchise?

7. Who was the voice of Shrek?

8. Lex and Tim were the children in which science fiction film?

9. Dustin Hoffman and Tom cruise starred together in which 1988 comedy drama?

10. What was the name of ET's friend?

ROUND 2: CHEMICAL SYMBOLS

1. Lead

2. Radon

3. Polonium

4. Uranium

5. Hafnium

6. Vandium

7. Gold

8. Mercury

9. Platinum

10. Hassium

ROUND 3: HISTORY

1. Emma Hamilton was the mistress of which leader?

2. Harland & Wolff constructed which famous vessel that sank?

3. Who was the youngest ever UK prime minister?

4. The ZX spectrum was invented by which person?

5. Dmitri Mendeleev created the first what?

6. In which century was Joan of Arc burnt at the stake?

7. Who succeeded Hitler?

8. The rock and ash from Mount Vesuvius destroyed which ancient city?

9. Jack Ruby became a famous name for shooting whom?

10. Elizabeth I and James I were the monarchs reigning when which bard was alive?

ROUND 4: COMPANY SLOGANS

1. Never knowingly undersold

2. Simples

3. The power of dreams

4. Always giving you extra

5. The world's local bank

6. You can do it, when you...

7. How do you eat yours?

8. It gives you wings

9. Should have gone to...?

10. Don't shop for it

ROUND 5: GEBERAL KNOWLEDGE

1. Juno was the Roman goddess of what?

2. What does the D stand for in HDMI?

3. In which county was Isaac Newton born?

4. Which country's motorway doesn't have a speed limit?

5. Xenophobia is a fear of what?

6. What is the birthstone of February?

7. Barney Rubble is cockney rhyming slang for what?

8. As of 2020, how many people have walked on the moon?

9. How many yards to a furlong?

10. Snake was the hero in which video game series?

ANAGRAM

Name the stage musical
from the anagram:
STEWY STEROIDS

CRYPTIC CLUE

Name the sports presenter
from the cryptic clue:
Prosecute yelper

LINKS

What links the following:
**Tony, Gordon, David,
Theresa**

Did You Know?

Each year, Finland hosts the
Mobile Phone Throwing
World Championships.
The record throw is over
110 metres.

Quiz 21

This was one of the most popular quizzes and most interacted with on social media.

ROUND 1: TV AND FILM

1. In which year did Who Wants to Be a Millionaire launch in the UK?

2. Diana Rigg and Honor Blackman have starred in which sixties TV series?

3. Which long running BBC comedy about a market trader from Peckham launched in 1981?

4. The Cigarette Smoking Man was a character in which TV series?

5. Simon Cowell produced his first ever BBC TV show launched in January 2019-what was the name?

6. Dr Strangelove, Goldfinger and A Hard Day's night were all released in which year?

7. In which film do a group of American kids stumble upon a treasure map purporting to lead to the famous pirate One Eyed Willy?

8. "Andy Dufresne who crawled through a river of s*** and came out clean on the other side", is a line from which nineties classic?

9. Vinny Jones, Brad Pitt and Jason Statham star in which film from the 2000s set around unlicensed boxing?

10. Name the film based on the life of Jordon Belfort released in 2013?

ROUND 2: SPORT

1. What is technically the maximum possible break in snooker?

2. Who has won the Ashes in cricket more times: England or Australia?

3. How many players are allowed on a court per team at any one time in a game of netball?

4. The most appearances in an FA Cup Final without winning it is 4, but who holds the record?

5. Since it became the six nations in 2000, two teams of the six have yet to win the tournament name one?

6. Cool Runnings and Eddie the Eagle were films based around which year's Winter Olympic games?

7. Which current Premier League venue has the biggest capacity?

8. Name the missing tournament: Wimbledon, Australian Open, French Open?

9. Jenson Button won his only F1 Title in 2009, but who was he driving for?

10. Which horse won the Grand National back to back in 2018 and 2019?

ROUND 3: MUSIC

1. Who sang It's Not Unusual in 1965?

2. The Foundation's 1968 Hit was called Build Me Up what?

3. Rivers of Babylon and Mary's Boy Child were seventies hits for which artist?

4. According to the Village People, where could you get clean, have a good meal and generally do what you feel?

5. Who was only halfway there, living on a prayer in 1986?

6. Who joined Queen to sing Under Pressure in 1981?

7. Britney Spears, Justin Timberlake and Christina Aguilera burst on to the music scene in the late nineties. But which American children's TV series did they all start on?

8. Which artists debut single was Because We Want To in 1998?

9. The Major needed help with this one... But who released the album Born to Do It in 2000?

10. The annoying and catchy song by Tones and I that hit number 1 in 2019, was called what?

ROUND 4: GEOGRAPHY

1. Which UK city would you associate with the Clifton Suspension Bridge?

2. China has the largest population in the world, but which country has the second largest?

3. Which is taller: the Eiffel Tower or Blackpool Tower?

4. What lies further to the West: John O'Groats or Blackpool?

5. How many countries border Switzerland?

6. The Channel Tunnel connects Calais and which UK town?

7. How many states are there in Australia?

8. Which island nation is just south of Florida?

9. How many of the 50 US states are not attached to the mainland?

10. What is the capital of Gibraltar?

ROUND 5: GEBERAL KNOWLEDGE

1. Dame Judi Dench appeared as "M" in how many James Bond films?

2. Which multimedia messaging app allows users to send messages and pictures that can disappear after being read, and create 24-hour stories?

3. What was Margaret Thatcher's middle name?

4. Which famous playwright died on 23rd April 1616?

5. In which century was St George chosen to be the patron saint of England?

6. Who was the sixth wife of Henry the eighth?

7. How many cards in total are there in the board game Cluedo?

8. In which country would you find Chernobyl?

9. MMXX is which year in Roman numerals?

10. Elon Musk is the current CEO of which car brand?

ANAGRAM

Name the children's book
character from the anagram:
INKY WALLOW

CRYPTIC CLUE

Name the London tube
station from the cryptic clue:
Battle sprint road

LINKS

What links the following:
**Georgia Toffolo, Stacey
Solomon, Gino D'Acampo,
Harry Redknapp**

Did You Know?

Only two mammals are
known to like spicy food:
humans and tree shrews.

Quiz 22

Another Saturday night with celebs posing the questions!

ROUND 1: TV AND FILM

1. What song does the main character wake up to every day in Groundhog Day?

2. Who was the first host of QI?

3. Velma Kelly and Roxie Hart star in which film?

4. What is the name of Postman Pat's cat?

5. How many boxes were used in the original Deal or No Deal?

6. Sebastian Croft played the younger version of which prominent character in Game Of Thrones?

7. The film 10 Things I Hate About You is based on which Shakespeare Play?

8. What was the first name of Bourne, played by Matt Damon?

9. What colour shorts does Bart Simpson wear?

10. Which pub name links the TV series Minder and the film Shaun of the Dead?

ROUND 2: SPORT AND LEISURE

1. In which game might you castle?

2. What is the value of the letter K in Scrabble?

3. What is the most valuable property on the UK monopoly board?

4. Which athletics event might you use the Fosbury flop?

5. How many players are there on a handball team?

6. Name a sporting team event where the winning team cross the line backwards?

7. How many numbers make up a roulette wheel?

8. In which sport do players sweep the ice?

9. What type of creature is Sonic?

10. Which oriental games is composed of 144 tiles?

ROUND 3: MUSIC

1. Brian McFadden left which boy band in 2004?

2. Bet You Look Good on the Dancefloor was a hit for which band?

3. Which band had members Michelle Williams, Kelly Rowland and Beyonce Knowles?

4. What kind of doll did Aqua sing about?

5. What was the Spice Girl's first single?

6. Which number 1 recording artist was pink, tall, spotted and very destructive?

7. Which British band became the first to headline Glastonbury 4 times?

8. Which BBC radio station banned the song Relax in the 80's?

9. Who was KC's Backing Band?

10. Apart from being number 1s, what do the Ballad of John and Yoko, Bohemian Rhapsody and **Space** Oddity have in common?

ROUND 4: SCIENCE AND NATURE

1. How many wings does a bee have?

2. Which is the lightest chemical element?

3. How many sides does an octagon have?

4. A chiropodist would treat which part of the body?

5. How many naturally occurring noble gases are there?

6. True or false, all bats are nocturnal?

7. What is the third planet from the sun called?

8. Which temperature has the same value in Celsius and Fahrenheit?

9. Au is the chemical symbol of which metal?

10. Which is the only fruit that grows its seeds on the outside?

ROUND 5: GEBERAL KNOWLEDGE

1. What is the age of criminal responsibility in the UK?

2. Which country gives a Christmas tree to Britain every year?

3. How many kings were there in a row between 1714 and 1820?

4. In which country was Julian Assange born?

5. Who is the artist responsible for creating the London Underground Labyrinth artwork?

6. In which country was Boris Johnson born?

7. Who makes the Model 3 and the model X cars?

8. Evita, Cats and Jesus Christ Superstar were musicals written by which composer?

9. Edward Elgar and Adam Smith have appeared on which banknote?

10. What was the name of the charity set up because a lady was too embarrassed to talk about her period?

ANAGRAM

Name the comedian from the anagram:

HANKY RETAINER

LINKS

What links the following:

Major Tom, Ziggy, Aladdin, Thin White Duke

CRYPTIC CLUE

Name the high street brand from the cryptic clue:

Log country

Did You Know?

In the Vatican, there is an ATM with instructions in Latin.

Quiz 23

ROUND 1: MUSIC

1. Who was the lead singer of Black Sabbath?

2. Justin, JC, Chris, Joey and Lance made up which boyband?

3. Who sang the original Shaft theme tune in 1971?

4. Kylie and Jason teamed up on which eighties duet?

5. Stay was a nineties hit for which artist?

6. Cotton Eye Joe was a hit for which nineties group?

7. Gareth Gates and the Kumars teamed up for which single in 2003?

8. Who joined Mark Ronson on the hit Valerie?

9. What year did Robbie Williams leave Take That?

10. What song did Brotherhood of Man sing at Eurovision?

ROUND 2: HISTORY

1. Who was on the throne when the Great Fire of London happened?

2. Which football club tragically lost players in the Munich air disaster?

3. Nancy Pelosi was the first female Speaker of what?

4. In 2010 the Burj Khalifa became what in the record books?

5. Rose Helibron became the first female judge to sit where in 1972?

6. In which month did the First World War begin?

7. What nationality was Sir Edmund Hillary?

8. Robert Walpole is considered to be the first British what?

9. The conquering of England is commemorated in which tapestry?

10. The communist government of Cuba was established by which leader?

ROUND 3: COMPANY SLOGANS

1. Life's for sharing

2. Power to you

3. It's so good I put my name on it

4. The make-up of make-up artists

5. Love the skin you're in

6. 8 out of 10 cats prefer it

7. It won't let you down

8. Master chocolatier

9. When's your day?

10. Live well for less

ROUND 4: MOVIES

1. What was the title of the 2019 Avengers Film?

2. Who played Jack in Titanic?

3. Who played Dominic Toretto in the Fast and the Furious franchise?

4. Who played James Bond in Skyfall?

5. What is the name of the hero cop in the Die Hard franchise?

6. Who voiced the genie in the animated film version of Aladdin?

7. Who played Queen Anne in the film The Favourite?

8. Who is Rocky's opponent in Rocky 2?

9. Who owned Greased Lightning in the film Grease?

10. Steven Spielberg directed which terrifying sea- related thriller?

ROUND 5: GEBERAL KNOWLEDGE

1. What does the S stand for in CSI?

2. In which country was Natalie Portman born?

3. Chronomentrophobia is a fear of what?

4. What is the oldest park in Central London?

5. Garnet is the birthstone for which month?

6. What Chinese zodiac sign comes after Rat?

7. What is the first book of the New Testament?

8. Trouble and strife is cockney rhyming slang for what?

9. According to Greek mythology who was the first woman on earth?

10. Michael, Trevor and Franklin were playable characters in which video Game?

ANAGRAM

Name the mountain range from the anagram:
YANK CONSORTIUM

CRYPTIC CLUE

Name the film from the cryptic clue:
My Italian mother

LINKS

What links the following:
Leeds United, Norwich City, Wolverhampton Wanderers, Newcastle United

Did You Know?

The English language did not originate in the British Isles. The local population spoke Celtic languages until Old English was brought over from mainland Europe by Anglo-Saxon settlers in the fifth century.

Quiz 24

ROUND 1: MOVIES

1. Who created the Star Wars franchise?

2. Who was the voice of Elsa in Frozen?

3. Frodo, Legolas and Gandalf were characters in which movie franchise?

4. Joaquin Phoenix portrayed which villain in the 2019 film of the same name?

5. Dead Man's Chest, At World's End and On Stranger Tides are movies in which franchise?

6. Who played President Whitmore in Independence day?

7. What was the name of the evil child in Toy Story?

8. Judgment Day was the strapline to which 1991 sci-fi movie?

9. Patrick Swayze, Demi Moore and Whoopi Goldberg starred in which 1990 movie?

10. Jerry Bruckheimer produced which 1986 US action drama film?

ROUND 2: NAME THE MANUFACTURER

1. Atom 3, Nomad

2. Alhambra, Ibiza

3. MX-5 CX-5

4. Civic, Accord

5. Juke, X-Trail

6. Golf, Polo

7. A5, Q7

8. XJ, XF

9. Discovery, Defender

10. I20, IX35

ROUND 3: HISTORY

1. In which month did the First World War end?

2. Who ascended the throne after Queen Victoria?

3. Which country was Robert Mugabe president of?

4. George Washington was the first president of which country?

5. Did Anne Boleyn really have 6 fingers?

6. On which day of the week did Titanic sink?

7. Which country was the first to give women the right to vote?

8. What was the surname of Clyde from the crime duo Bonnie and Clyde?

9. "For Valour" are the words inscribed into which medal?

10. Who was said to have rode naked through the streets of Coventry in the 11th century?

ROUND 4: UK TOURIST ATTRACTIONS WHICH COUNTY?

1. Stonehenge

2. National Coal Mining Museum

3. Blackpool Tower

4. Angel of the North

5. Loch Ness

6. Roman Baths

7. Eden Project

8. Shakespeare's Birthplace

9. Cheddar Gorge

10. Chester Zoo

ROUND 5: GEBERAL KNOWLEDGE

1. Mars was the Roman god of what?

2. What does the L stand for in laser?

3. In which American state was Barack Obama born?

4. Microphobia is the fear of what?

5. Diamond is the birthstone for which month?

6. What was the name of Tonto's horse?

7. Dog and bone is cockney rhyming slang for what?

8. How many points are needed to win a game of cribbage?

9. Barbara Millicent Roberts is better known by which name?

10. Which game company made the FIFA game series?

ANAGRAM

Name the English footballer
from the anagram:
MERE EARTHLINGS

CRYPTIC CLUE

Name the UK city from the
cryptic clue:
Fresh fortress

LINKS

What links the following:
**Martin, Buckland,
Berryman, Champion**

Did You Know?

In 2016, Domino's Pizza
in Japan started training
reindeer to deliver
takeaways during the
snowy winter season.
They dropped the plans
shortly afterwards.

Quiz 25

ROUND 1: MUSIC

1. Who was the lead singer of Blondie?

2. Who had a 1964 hit with You Really Got Me?

3. What did Wizard want to see jive in 1973?

4. What kind of love did Soft Cell sing about in the eighties hit?

5. How many limits were there in the song by 2 Unlimited?

6. According to his noughties hit, what kind of day was Daniel Powter having?

7. According to the title of her song, what was Adele rolling in?

8. What is Freddy Mercury's real name?

9. Who won the first series of Fame Academy?

10. What was the name of Love City Groove Eurovision song?

ROUND 2: GEOGRAPHY

1. What is the largest lake by area contained in one country?

2. Aconcagua mountain is in which country?

3. How many emirates make up the United Arab Emirates?

4. Fort Knox is in which US state?

5. For a Scottish mountain to be called a munro, it must be above how many feet?

6. Persia is the former name for which country?

7. Which country has the longest coastline?

8. Which country contains the largest number of active volcanoes?

9. SOU is the airport code for which airport?

10. If you sail due east from New York, which European country would you hit first?

ROUND 3: HISTORY

1. General Eisenhower commanded the Allied forces on which Key day in World War II?

2. 1936 saw which king abdicate?

3. The Iron Age came after which age?

4. Where in the US held the famous Tea Party in 1773?

5. Ramsey McDonald formed the first Labour what in 1924?

6. Merlin was an advisor to which king?

7. What is the oldest university in the USA?

8. John Adams was the first president to live in which building?

9. The Wars of the Roses took place in which century?

10. Orson Welles' radio broadcast of what show caused Americans to panic in 1938?

ROUND 4: CONNECTIONS ROUND

1. What is the only mammal with wings?

2. The first name of the England goalkeeper banks?

3. A brand that specialises in surf and sports-related apparel?

4. The season after autumn?

5. A word that can follow, thunder, snow and rain?

6. The largest mammal of the procyonid family native to North America?

7. The largest of the arachnid family?

8. Who is said to generally go down with the ship?

9. Fe is the chemical symbol for what?

10. What links all the answers?

ROUND 5: GEBERAL KNOWLEDGE

1. Flora was the Roman goddess of what?

2. What does the S stand for in NASCAR?

3. In which country was Keanu Reeves born?

4. Entomophobia is the fear of what?

5. Emerald is the birthstone for which month?

6. What comes after Genesis in the Bible?

7. Mutt and Jeff is cockney rhyming slang for what?

8. What is the name of the female character in the Tomb Raider series?

9. Aglet is the name of what part of a shoe?

10. Which company makes instant printing cameras?

ANAGRAM

Name the large predator from the anagram:
COOL DICER

LINKS

What links the following:
Germany, Austro-Hungarian Empire, Bulgaria, Ottoman Empire

CRYPTIC CLUE

Name the TV presenter from the cryptic clue:
Target above houses

Did You Know?

The longest international cricket match ever played was South Africa vs England in 1939. It lasted more than 12 days and was called off because England would otherwise have missed the boat home.

Quiz 26

ROUND 1: ACRONYMS

1. What does the S stand for in NASA?

2. What does the L stand for in BLT?

3. What does the Q stand for in NASDAQ?

4. What does the S stand for in HSBC?

5. What does the Q stand for in IQ?

6. What does the A stand for in ATM?

7. What does the I stand for in ISBN?

8. What does the T stand for in SWAT?

9. What does the WD stand for in WD-40?

10. What does the Y stand for in YMCA?

ROUND 2: MOVIES

1. Who wrote Love Actually?

2. What was the name of the character Richard Gere played in Pretty Woman?

3. Molly Ringwald played Andie Walsh in which 1986 teen romantic comedy?

4. In which film does Bill Murray keep reliving the same day?

5. Who plays Rod Tidwell in Jerry Maguire?

6. Brad Pitt and Angelina Jolie star in Mr and Mrs what?

7. What type of singer does Adam Sandler play in the film of the same name?

8. Pierce Brosnan, Colin Firth and Stellan Skarsgaard play potential fathers in which Movie?

9. Amy Adams plays Giselle in which 2007 Disney romantic musical?

10. Yesterday is a film where there character wakes up and finds out which band never existed?

ROUND 3: TV

1. Nancy Cartwright is the voice of which animated character?

2. Nicholas Lyndhurst played which character in Only Fools and Horses?

3. The former presenters of which BBC show created The Grand Tour on Amazon Prime?

4. Charlie Fairhead is a character in which TV drama?

5. In which American TV series would you find Luke's Diner?

6. Lifeguards is the central job in which TV series?

7. Sharon and Tracey were sisters in which TV series?

8. Simon Templar was the alter ego of which character?

9. What is Dec of Ant and Dec's surname?

10. Where is Fawlty Towers set?

ROUND 4: SPORT

1. Maradona's hand of god happened in which year?

2. What is the first name of the legendary F1 commentator Mr Walker?

3. Former England cricket captain Nasser Hussain was born in which country?

4. In which athletics discipline is a planting box required?

5. What nationality is Graeme Souness?

6. Potting the green ball in snooker gets you how many points?

7. What pieces line-up at the front row in a game of chess?

8. Which boxer received the first knighthood?

9. Will Carling was England captain in which sport?

10. Sid Waddell was a commentator in which sport?

ROUND 5: GEBERAL KNOWLEDGE

1. What does the B stand for in BMW?

2. In which country was Emma Watson born?

3. What is Postman Pat's son called?

4. Hypochondria is the fear of what?

5. Aquamarine is the birthstone for which month?

6. What is the last book of the Old Testament?

7. Who was Mario trying to rescue in Super Mario Bros?

8. In slang terms, what amount is a monkey?

9. Which is the largest of the Channel Islands?

10. Who is the lead singer of the Kaiser Chiefs?

ANAGRAM

Name the singer
from the anagram:
EARED HENS

CRYPTIC CLUE

Name the song from
the cryptic clue:
Prod her features

LINKS

What links the following:
**Ann, Branwell, Emily,
Charlotte**

Did You Know?

The scientific name
for the Western lowland
gorilla is "gorilla
gorilla gorilla".

Quiz 27

ROUND 1: GEOGRAPHY

1. What is the official language of Chile?

2. Mecca is in which country?

3. The Bering Strait is between Alaska and which country?

4. The source of the river Niagara comes from which lake?

5. Which country is the rising point for the Amazon?

6. Which river flows North and South of the Equator?

7. Cowes can be found on which island?

8. Which country is Easter Island a dependency of?

9. Tbilisi is the capital of which country?

10. The headquarters of Interpol are in which European city?

ROUND 2: GUESS THE YEAR (+/- 2 YEARS FOR THE POINT)

1. The Gunpowder Plot

2. The Bank of England is founded

3. Tower Bridge opens

4. Foundation of the BBC

5. Queen Elizabeth II ascends the throne

6. Britain joins the EEC

7. The Berlin Wall comes down

8. Britain hands back Hong Kong

9. Orville and Wilbur Wright's first flight

10. The D-Day landings

ROUND 3: HISTORY

1. Luftwaffe was the name of which country's air force during World War II?

2. What comes after the Stone Age?

3. Anne Boleyn and Catherine Howard were both executed where?

4. Which ocean did Amelia Earhart disappear over?

5. Who was UK prime minister at the start of World War II?

6. How long did the 100 Years' War last?

7. Boxing day and which saint share the 26th December?

8. What was the name of the ancient Jewish manuscripts found between 1946 and 1956?

9. What was the name given to the person said to have murdered five prostitutes in 1888?

10. Alfred Nobel is best known for inventing what?

ROUND 4: TV

1. What is the real name of the Vixen on The Chase?

2. Julian Fellowes created which historical TV drama?

3. Jodie Comer and Sandra Oh are the lead actresses on which TV series?

4. Who plays Rita Sullivan in Coronation Street?

5. What was the name of the bar where everyone knows your name?

6. Noel Fielding co-presents which cooking-related show?

7. Lee Mack stars in which BBC sitcom?

8. Who presents 8 Out of 10 Cats Does Countdown?

9. What is Bart Simpson's full name?

10. Gobo, Mokey, Red, Wembley and Boober where characters in which TV series?

ROUND 5: GEBERAL KNOWLEDGE

1. Theology is the study of what?

2. Filibeg is the traditional Scottish word for what?

3. What does TT stand for in Isle of Man TT racing?

4. How many yards must an opposition player stand back from a free kick in football?

5. The famous Zebra Crossing on which street has been given heritage status?

6. The Viral 2014 Ice Bucket Challenge was created to promote awareness and raise money for which disease?

7. What does PDF stand for?

8. What is the criss-cross pattern on top of a pie called?

9. What was Nigel Benn's nickname?

10. In which country did David and Victoria Beckham marry?

ANAGRAM

Name the Shakespeare
play from the anagram:
TEMPT SHEET

CRYPTIC CLUE

Name the car manufacturer
from the cryptic clue:
Sprint on your backside

LINKS

What links the following:
**7/11, Irreplaceable, Diva,
Halo**

Did You Know?

There is a Starbucks
coffee cup visible in
every scene of the 1999
film Fight Club.

Quiz 28

ROUND 1: MUSIC

1. Chrissie Hynde was a singer in which group?

2. T-Boz, Lisa "Left Eye" Lopes and Rozonda "Chilli" Thomas made up which girl group?

3. Who recorded the 1960 song My Old Man's a Dustman?

4. What did Stevie Wonder call to say according to the eighties hit?

5. Take My Breath Away featured on which eighties movie?

6. Who sang the song Men In Black?

7. Call On Me was a hit for which artist in the noughties?

8. Hey There Delilah was a 2006 hit for which group?

9. Who was Dancing On My Own according to the title of their 2016 hit?

10. Who was the last UK winner of Eurovision?

ROUND 2: ART AND LITERATURE

1. Goneril, Regan and Cordelia are characters in which Shakespeare play?

2. Ernest Hemingway wrote The Old Man and the what?

3. Which was the first James Bond novel to be published by Ian Fleming?

4. How old was Adrian Mole when he wrote his secret diary?

5. What animal was Jeremy Fisher in the Beatrix Potter tales?

6. "All children, except one, grow up", is the opening line to which book?

7. Who wrote the poem Paradise Lost?

8. Who wrote The Woman in Black?

9. What type of creature was Aragog in the Harry Potter books?

10. Andrew Motion was Poet what between 1999 and 2009?

ROUND 3: NAME THE MANUFACTURER

1. Boxter, Cayenne

2. Avensis, Aygo

3. Fortwo, Forfour

4. 9-3, 9-5

5. Avenger, Caliber

6. Captiva, Spark

7. Edge, Galaxy

8. Elise, Exige

9. QX50, QX70

10. Sorento, Sedona

ROUND 4: SPORT

1. What is the hymn sung before the FA Cup final?

2. Freestyle and Greco are types of what?

3. Eight ball, nine ball and straight are types of what?

4. A zamboni resurfaces which surface?

5. Who was nicknamed the "Whirlwind" in snooker?

6. A final play Hail Mary is found in which American sport?

7. What is the diameter in inches of a golf hole?

8. In which sport would you find a face-off?

9. Lennox Lewis was beaten for the first time by which boxer?

10. Who was the first recorded person to swim the channel?

ROUND 5: GEBERAL KNOWLEDGE

1. How much is Old Kent Road to buy on a standard Monopoly board?

2. Who narrated the Harry Potter audiobooks in the UK?

3. What is the longest motorway in the UK?

4. Which band's songs are used as the theme tunes to the CSI series?

5. What do the letters DC stand for in Washington DC?

6. What is taller: the Crystal Palace Transmitter or the London Eye?

7. In Sing a Song of Sixpence, how many blackbirds were baked in a pie?

8. In Downton Abbey, Hugh Bonneville plays which character?

9. Which is further west, Edinburgh or Bristol?

10. Ryder, Chase and Marshall are characters in which children's TV Series?

ANAGRAM

Name the European city from the anagram:

LEAN COBRA

CRYPTIC CLUE

Name the tree from the cryptic clue:

Might tug

LINKS

What links the following:

Dionysus, Ares, Demeter, Artemis

Did You Know?

Shakira was rejected from her school choir because her teacher said she sang like a goat.

Quiz 29

ROUND 1: MUSIC

1. Robert Plant was the lead singer of which band?

2. Let's Twist Again was a 1961 hit for whom?

3. When You're In Love With A Beautiful Woman was a 1979 hit for which doctor?

4. Yazz said the only way was what?

5. Coolio sang about gangsters' what in the nineties?

6. Which reality competition winner's debut single was All This Time?

7. Happy was a hit for which artist in 2014?

8. Who had a number 1 single in each decade from the 50s to the 90s?

9. Who sang Ooh Aah...Just a Little Bit at Eurovision?

10. Which band was created through the reality TV series Popstars?

ROUND 2: SPORT

1. Gareth Bale left which club to sign for Real Madrid?

2. After a tyre dispute due to fears over safety, how many cars lined up on the grid at the 2005 US Grand Prix?

3. In cricket, if the ball bounces before it crosses the boundary rope, how many runs are scored?

4. Which London-based Rugby Super League team was relegated at the end of the 2019 season?

5. The French Open is played on what surface?

6. Clean & jerk and the snatch are synonymous with which sport?

7. King of the mountain in the Tour de France has what kind of jersey?

8. In which year was the Grand National run on the Monday after a bomb threat caused the race to be postponed?

9. In game of croquet, how many hoops are used?

10. What number is a perfect game in ten-pin bowling?

ROUND 3: HISTORY

1. Who did the USA buy Alaska from?

2. What was the name given to the Local Defence Volunteer?

3. Mike Pence was the running mate for which US president?

4. Sir Walter Raleigh is said to have placed his cloak on a puddle for which British monarch?

5. Along with his wife Catherine, what organisation did William Booth found?

6. On what date is St Patrick's day celebrated?

7. Which country's civil war broke out in 1936?

8. The Crystal Palace originally stood in which London Park?

9. Edward VIII abdicated to marry whom?

10. The Guinness Book of Records went on sale for the first time ever in which decade?

ROUND 4: CAPITAL CITIES

1. Canberra

2. Nairobi

3. Valetta

4. Pyongyang

5. Warsaw

6. Jakarta

7. Budapest

8. Nicosia

9. Zagreb

10. Ottawa

ROUND 5: GEBERAL KNOWLEDGE

1. The Richter scale measures the intensity of what?

2. In which modern-day country did the Battle of Waterloo take place?

3. Leigh-Anne, Jesy, Jade and Perrie make up which girl band?

4. In Netball, what does GA stand for?

5. In Despicable Me, who is the boss of the Minions?

6. Which opened to the public first, the London Eye or the Millennium Dome?

7. Scoop, Muck and Dizzy are characters in which children's TV show?

8. What is the name of the star closest to us?

9. Worthy Farm is the usual home of which festival?

10. What is the official language of the USA?

ANAGRAM

Name the classic film from the anagram:
SEMI TOOTHLIKE

LINKS

What links the following:
Robert Galbraith, George Eliot, Andy Stack, Ellis Bell

CRYPTIC CLUE

Name the children's author from the cryptic clue:
Lager cons ceramics maker

Did You Know?

The Eiffel Tower was originally meant to be built in Barcelona, but the locals rejected it because they thought it would be an eyesore.

Quiz 30

ROUND 1: TV

1. LL Cool J was the host of which celebrity singing battle?

2. James Gordon and Barbara Kean were central characters in which TV series?

3. In the TV show Take Me Out, male contestants appear on stage via what?

4. What was the name of the coach driver in Coach Trip?

5. Who was the first head chef of Hell's Kitchen in the UK?

6. The fictional police station of Gasforth was the setting for which sit-com?

7. I'm Always Here was the name of the theme tune to which nineties American drama?

8. Dinner Ladies was created, written and starred in by which actress?

9. Woodentop was the name of the pilot episode for which long-running TV drama?

10. "Don't tell him your name, Pike" was a famous line from which TV series?

ROUND 2: SPORT

1. The Community Shield is played between the winner of the FA Cup and the winner of which other competition?

2. Who is the only driver to achieve the triple crown in motorsport?

3. Can a player get out on a no ball in cricket?

4. Who coached England to Rugby World Cup victory in 2003?

5. Roland Garros is the other name for which tennis Grand Slam tournament?

6. What colour are the two outer rings in archery?

7. What do you call a boxer who leads with his right?

8. The bed of a snooker table is made from what?

9. How many people are traditionally on a tug-of-war team?

10. Roger Bannister was the first person to run what?

ROUND 3: GUESS THE YEAR

1. Margaret Thatcher became leader of the Conservative party?

2. Trevor Francis became the world's first million pound footballer?

3. World record breaking Virtual Pub Quiz host Jay Flynn was born?

4. Nelson Mandela was freed from prison?

5. Take That split up?

6. Prince Harry was born?

7. Walt Disney's Fantasia is released?

8. the Eurozone and the International Monetary Fund agreed a 110 billion euro bailout deal for Greece

9. John Lennon was forced to apologise for claiming that the Beatles were "more popular than Jesus".

10. The formation of the United Nations?

ROUND 4: MOVIE TAGLINES

1. She doesn't give an F

2. The true story of a real fake

3. Don't get mad, get everything

4. Even a hitman deserves a second chance

5. Trust me

6. Nice planet, we'll take it

7. You won't believe your eye

8. Makes Ben Hur look like an epic

9. A romantic comedy, with zombies

10. Love is in the hair

ROUND 5: GEBERAL KNOWLEDGE

1. What was the name of the cowboy in Toy Story?

2. The Bullring shopping centre can be found in which UK City?

3. What does the R stand for in ANPR?

4. Which actor links the cartoon characters Danger Mouse and Count Duckula?

5. The ballroom, the study and the kitchen are all rooms in which board game?

6. Which comedian changed his name to Hugo Boss, and has since changed it back?

7. In the fairy tales, who left a trail of breadcrumbs to find their way home?

8. The Vatican City is completely surrounded by which country?

9. Which small island sits to the west of Barrow-in-Furness and the east of Northern Ireland?

10. Tony Stark is the alter ego of which superhero?

ANAGRAM

Name the celebrity chef from the anagram:
SHIRTY ALIENATOR

LINKS

What links the following:
Australia, France, UK, US

CRYPTIC CLUE

Name the London tube station from the cryptic clue:
Lipstick mix street

Did You Know?

Baby elephants often suck their trunks for comfort.

Quiz 31

ROUND 1: MUSIC

1. Who was the lead singer of Aerosmith?

2. AJ, Howie, Nick, Kevin and Brian made up which boy band?

3. Wooden Heart and Surrender were hits for which American singer?

4. School's Out was a hit for which artist in 1972?

5. Ride On Time was a hit for which group in the eighties?

6. Baddiel and Skinner teamed up with which band on Three Lions?

7. Tony Christie teamed up with which comedian for the re-release of Amarillo?

8. Which artist re-entered the charts in 2010 with their hit Don't Stop Believin'?

9. Dua Lipa teamed up with whom on the 2018 hit One Kiss?

10. Patricia Bredin represented the UK in which event?

ROUND 2: CAPITALS

1. Oslo

2. Tunis

3. Port of Spain

4. Damascus

5. Bern

6. Seoul

7. Freetown

8. Moscow

9. Kathmandu

10. Wellington

ROUND 3: HISTORY

1. Reims was the French city where which country's surrender was signed?

2. Which Astronaut stayed behind in the command capsule when the other two set foot on the moon?

3. Who was Queen Elizabeth I's mother?

4. To Kill a Mockingbird was released in which year?

5. What was the name of the German Coding machine used in World War II?

6. What was the surname of Bonnie from the crime duo Bonnie and Clyde?

7. Hiroshima was the first city in history to have what dropped on it?

8. The first English translation of the Bible was written in which century?

9. Who appeared on the first ever cover of Playboy magazine?

10. What is the oldest USA state?

ROUND 4: ART AND LITERATURE

1. What is the first name of the Harry Potter author?

2. What is the name of Sherlock Holme's Brother?

3. Who wrote The Godfather?

4. According to legend, Guinevere was married to which king?

5. Whose autobiography is Dreams From My Father?

6. Which artist cut off most of his ear?

7. Sir Christopher Wren designed which cathedral?

8. Who painted the Dogs Playing Poker paintings?

9. In the song, who killed Cock Robin?

10. A Christmas Carol is set in which city?

ROUND 5: GEBERAL KNOWLEDGE

1. In the song Baby Shark, which shark comes after grandma shark?

2. Elpheba is a witch in which musical?

3. Scrappy is the nephew of which cartoon character?

4. Which European river flows through 10 different countries?

5. A royal flush is the best possible hand in which card game?

6. What is the third letter of the Greek alphabet?

7. What is the name of Dennis the Menace's dog?

8. What size of paper typically measures 21 by 30 cm?

9. In radio, what does the M stand for in FM?

10. In which month in the UK is the longest day?

ANAGRAM

Name the British film
star from the anagram:
OPEN MAMMOTHS

CRYPTIC CLUE

Name the UK town
from the cryptic clue:
Finished hard dash

LINKS

What links the following:
**Roger, John, Freddie,
Brian**

Did You Know?

The tallest mountain in
the world is Mauna Kea
in Hawaii at over 33,000
feet. It is more than 3,000
feet taller than Mount
Everest, but most of
it is below sea level.

Quiz 32

ROUND 1: MUSIC

1. Keith, Stephen, Michael, Ronan and Shane made up which boyband?

2. Which music artist was part of Scream, Nirvana and Foo Fighters?

3. Sonny and Cher released which duet in 1965?

4. Who released Bohemian Rhapsody in 1975?

5. Elaine Paige and which artist teamed up on the song I Know Him So Well?

6. Children was a hit in the nineties for whom?

7. That's My Goal was a 2006 debut hit for which artist?

8. Who stormed into the charts with her hit Bad Guy?

9. How many times have the UK won Eurovision?

10. Which group sung about Massachusetts in 1967?

ROUND 2: GUESS THE YEAR

1. Abba won the Eurovision song contest

2. Concorde took off for its maiden passenger flight

3. Return of the Jedi was released in cinemas

4. The space shuttle Challenger exploded

5. The Full Monty was released in cinemas

6. Blackpool Tower first opened

7. President John F Kennedy was assassinated

8. Harold Wilson resigned as Prime Minister

9. George V became King of England

10. America declared independence from Great Britain

ROUND 3: TV

1. Who played the grandson of Norman Stanley Fletcher in the 2016 reboot of Porridge?

2. What was the short lived prequel to Only Fools and Horses called?

3. Which magician performed Russian Roulette live in 2003?

4. Martin Sheen and Rob Lowe starred in which American political drama?

5. Bayside High was the setting for which TV show?

6. Mulder and Scully were detectives in which TV drama?

7. 'Allo 'Allo was set in which war?

8. Complete the TV show title, It Ain't Half?

9. Sodor and Knapford were train stations in which children's TV series?

10. Chatsworth council estate was the setting for which TV series?

ROUND 4: SPORT

1. Leicester, Manchester United and Tottenham are the only teams to score how many in a single Premier League match?

2. In what year did Ayrton Senna die?

3. A maiden over in cricket means how many runs were conceded?

4. How many points is a conversion worth in rugby union?

5. Tennis star Martina Hingis came from which country?

6. What do runners pass from hand to hand in a relay race?

7. Which four-legged sporting icon died in October 1995 aged 30?

8. In what sport might you need the spider rest?

9. Audley Harrison won which boxing medal at the 2000 Olympics?

10. Shortstop is a fielding position in which sport?

ROUND 5: GEBERAL KNOWLEDGE

1. On which island was Napoleon Bonaparte born?

2. What is the longest river in Europe?

3. What did John Logie Baird invent in 1925?

4. Pentonville Road is how much in Monopoly?

5. What is an archer's arrow case called?

6. Which British radio DJ's nickname was "Fluff"?

7. In which year was the MOT test introduced in the UK?

8. Who is the Greek god of music?

9. Which US city hosted the 1985 Live Aid concert?

10. What is belladonna commonly known as?

ANAGRAM

Name the type of tree
from the anagram:
SOUTHERN CHEST

LINKS

What links the following:
**Lincoln, Garfield,
McKinley, Kennedy**

CRYPTIC CLUE

Name the high street brand
from the cryptic clue:
Big white vehicles

Did You Know?

The longest wedding veil
in recorded history
was the length of
66 football pitches.

Quiz 33

ROUND 1: CARS -NAME THE MANUFACTURER

1. Adam, Corsa

2. 124 Spider, 595

3. Levante, Quattroporte

4. D-Max, Rodeo

5. Ghost, Phantom

6. Swift, Ignis

7. Impreza, Forester

8. Partner Tepee, RCZ

9. Gallardo, Aventador

10. Bentayga, Continental

ROUND 2: SPORT

1. As of 2020, what is the best place the England Women's Football World Cup team have managed to achieve?

2. What nationality is a former F1 World Champion Jacques Villeneuve?

3. How many overs are bowled by each side on a one day match in cricket?

4. What is the first name of the former rugby league player Offiah?

5. What nationality is tennis star Andy Roddick?

6. Which rings are worth more points in archery, red or blue?

7. Red and what other colour alternate on the smallest segments on a dart board?

8. What nationality is Stephen Hendry?

9. What is the last event of the heptathlon?

10. The lightest ball is used in which sport?

ROUND 3: TV

1. Sophie Turner, Kit Harrington and Maisie Williams starred in which 2010s smash hit TV show?

2. Who plays the president of the United States in the Netflix TV series Designated Survivor?

3. Ross Kemp starred in which SAS-based drama running for 4 series?

4. Geraldine was the name of the vicar in which TV show?

5. The Sacred Heart Hospital is the setting for which TV show?

6. Which American cartoon created by Seth MacFarlane launched in 1999?

7. Complete the TV show title Whose line is it...?

8. "And it's good night from him", was a closing line from which TV show?

9. Arnold Rimmer was a hologram in which TV Comedy?

10. Complete the TV show title: The Brittas...?

ROUND 4: GEOGRAPHY

1. What is the oldest city in the world?

2. Which US state has the most active volcanoes?

3. What is the largest country in the Arabian peninsula?

4. What is the largest country in South America by land area?

5. Which mountain is known by the name Savage Mountain?

6. Which is the only continent that has land in all four hemispheres?

7. What is the name of the active volcano on earth

8. Kuala Lumpur is the capital city of which country?

9. What is the name of the body of water that separates Europe and Africa?

10. Not including the Polar deserts, which is the largest desert in the world?

ROUND 5: GEBERAL KNOWLEDGE

1. Marsh Gas is another name for what gas?

2. How much is Bow Street on a monopoly board?

3. What is the name of the official residence of the Lord Mayor of London?

4. What is the collective noun for a group of beavers?

5. How many carats is pure gold?

6. Cartomancy is fortune-telling using what?

7. Which insect lives in a formicary?

8. What type of flower is a lady's slipper?

9. What is the wife of a Marquess?

10. What is the brightest star in the night sky?

ANAGRAM

Name the fictional detective
from the anagram:
MORE SHELLSHOCK

CRYPTIC CLUE

Name the film from
the cryptic clue:
My horrible self

LINKS

What links the following:
**Cheshire, Shropshire,
Herefordshire,
Gloucestershire**

Did You Know?

In the Second World
War, a brown bear
called Wojtek was
officially enlisted in the
Polish army and was
subsequently promoted
to corporal.

Quiz 34

ROUND 1: MUSIC

1. Who was the lead singer of No Doubt?

2. She Loves You, Please Please Me and A Hard Day's Night were hits for whom?

3. Complete the Mungo Jerry song, In The...?

4. How many times a lady did Commodores sing about?

5. What did T'Pau have in their hand according to the title of the song?

6. Think Twice was a nineties hit for whom?

7. Sugababes wanted to push what according to the title of their song?

8. What Makes You Beautiful was a 2012 hit for which boyband?

9. What was the name of the singing competition that Will Young won?

10. Love Will Set You Free was a UK Eurovision entry for which artist?

ROUND 2: SPORT

1. Blackburn Rovers, Leicester City and Liverpool have each won which tournament once?

2. Albert Park is the setting for which country's F1 Race?

3. How many arms does an umpire put in the air to signal a 6 in cricket?

4. How many points is a try worth in Rugby union?

5. How many tournaments make up the golf Grand Slam?

6. Which rugby Super League side has won the challenge cup the most times?

7. Who was the first darts player to receive and MBE?

8. The heptathlon starts with which event?

9. The Marquess of Queensberry rules, are a code of generally accepted rules in which sport?

10. How many players are allowed to score in netball?

ROUND 3: TV

1. The Stig is a tame racing driver from which TV series?

2. Tim Lovejoy and Simon Rimmer present which Sunday Morning cooking show?

3. Complete the Marvel TV Series title, Agents of ?

4. Band of Brothers was created by Steven Spielberg and which A-list actor?

5. Walter White was the lead character in which TV series?

6. Sheldon, Leonard and Penny were characters in which TV show?

7. What was the name of the hospital in Casualty?

8. What was the name of the tower block that Del Boy and Rodney lived in?

9. Complete the title of the TV show: To The Manor...?

10. Corbett and Barker made up which comedy duo?

ROUND 4: ART AND LITERATURE

1. Emilia, Dedemona and Iago are characters in which Shakespeare play?

2. The area of stage furthest from the audience is known by what name?

3. The dance of the fandango originates from which country?

4. Is the Venus de Milo a painting or a sculpture?

5. Who wrote The Man in the Iron Mask?

6. What was the name of the disciple who betrayed Jesus to the Romans?

7. Who was married to William Shakespeare between 1582 and his death in 1616?

8. Who painted Les Parapluies?

9. What was the title of British author Salman Rushdie's controversial 1988 novel?

10. Who is a danseur?

ROUND 5: GEBERAL KNOWLEDGE

1. What are Latter Day Saints otherwise known as?

2. What is a puppet worked by strings called?

3. The secret ingredient of which product is code-named "merchandise 7X"?

4. What is the tenth letter of the Greek alphabet?

5. In what country is the Valley of the Kings?

6. How many lines are in a limerick?

7. Trinitrotoluene is better known as what?

8. What is the human ailment epistaxis better known as?

9. Assassinated in 1965, who was Malcolm Little better known as?

10. In the human body, in which organ would you find the Loop of Henle?

ANAGRAM

Name the video game
from the anagram:
TAUNT GODFATHER

CRYPTIC CLUE

Name the song from
the cryptic clue:
Prison residence stone

LINKS

What links the following:
**Dawn of the Dinosaurs,
Continental Drift,
Collision Course, The
Meltdown**

Did You Know?

Between North and
South Korea there is 155
miles of no man's land
that provides a habitat
for hundreds of rare
animal species.

Quiz 35

ROUND 1: MUSIC

1. Bananarama were an eighties female group from which country?

2. Anyone Who Had a Heart and You're My World was hits for which Liverpudlian singer?

3. What was going to stop Starship in the eighties according to the title of the song?

4. According to his nineties hit, what was Chesney Hawkes?

5. What did James Bay want to hold back according to the title of his 2015 hit?

6. Bonnie Tyler sang which song in her 2013 Eurovision appearance?

7. Good Vibrations was a hit for which group in 1966?

8. What was Prince's favourite colour?

9. Who was Kung Fu Fighting in 1974?

10. Which TV singing contest allowed members of the public to impersonate their favourite artists?

ROUND 2: SPORT

1. Which player missed a penalty in the semi-final against Germany at euro 96?

2. Who won the 1994 F1 World Championship despite crashing into Damon Hill?

3. Over how many days is a test match usually played in cricket?

4. As of 2020, which female tennis player has won the most Wimbledon singles titles?

5. In 1995, who was the first player in the tennis open era to be disqualified from Wimbledon?

6. In which golf tournament is the winner presented with the Green Jacket?

7. In ice hockey, which is the only player allowed to use their feet?

8. A touchdown is worth how many points in American Football?

9. What is the length of an Olympic-sized swimming pool?

10. Which Australian city is the host of the Australian tennis open?

ROUND 3: TV

1. David Schwimmer and Nick Mohammed starred in which Sky 1 comedy?

2. Who played Dr Watson in Sherlock?

3. Complete the title of the Netflix show set in the eighties, Stranger?

4. John Simm, Bill Nighy and James McAvoy all starred in which noughties political drama series?

5. Which actor played doctor Gregory House in the American medical drama?

6. Insomnia Café was the working title for which long running TV sitcom?

7. What was the name of the BBC Saturday morning children's TV show running from 1993-2001?

8. In which children's TV show did a boy have a watch that could stop time?

9. Aunts Zelda and Hilda and cat Salem were characters in which nineties TV series?

10. Adrian Edmondson and Rik Mayall starred in which 1982-84 TV comedy?

ROUND 4: GEOGRAPHY

1. Where is the largest volcano in the world?

2. What is the most populous continent?

3. What is the most populous city in the world?

4. How many stars are there on the Australian flag?

5. The Sahara desert can be found in which country?

6. Acapulco is a city in which country?

7. The Manat is a currency in which country?

8. What is the world's most and neutral country?

9. Mount Olympus is the highest mountain in which country?

10. Portugal can be found as part of which peninsula?

ROUND 5: GEBERAL KNOWLEDGE

1. What element is mixed with iron to make cast iron?

2. Where on a woman's body would you see a bindi?

3. Who, in 1990, became the first chancellor of a united Germany?

4. What is the nineties cult Japanese electronic toy which is cared for as if it were a pet?

5. Who was the first woman to win a Nobel Prize?

6. What colour is the letter L in the standard Google logo?

7. What is the popular name for little baked sausages wrapped in rashers of streaky bacon?

8. What is the fourth letter of the Greek alphabet?

9. Eric Cartman is a character in which cartoon series?

10. A "pea-souper" is which type of weather condition?

ANAGRAM

Name the herb from the anagram:
REPLAYS

LINKS

What links the following:
Mickey Dolenz, Davy Jones, Peter Tork, Mike Nesmith

CRYPTIC CLUE

Name the musical instrument from the cryptic clue:
Urinate a negative

Did You Know?

In Israel, it is illegal to bring a bear to the beach.

Readers' Round

By Chris Butler

1. What was the first song on the first Now That's What I Call Music album?

By Lucy Dowle

2. In which country is it illegal to own just one guinea pig?

By Dan Moston

3. What is the oldest uniformed youth organisation in the world? a) The Scouts or b) The Boys' Brigade?

By Nicole Mercedes

4. What is the most common colour of toilet paper in France?

By Lauren Fowler

5. In the film Gremlins, what are the three important rules that must not be broken when looking after a Mogwai?

By Liz Husband

6. Where in everyday life would you find the words "Standing on the shoulders of giants"?

By Adam Dempsey

7. What food can be made from combining the chemical symbols for Boron, Actinium, Oxygen and Nitrogen?

By Corrina Wilson

8. What are there "virtually" (see what I did there) none of in New Zealand?

By Philippa Taylor-Gadd

9. What was the first frozen vegetable available in the UK?

By Tim Blissett

10. How many rooms are there in Buckingham Palace?

By Charlotte Zhivago

11. On the Beaufort wind scale, which number represents a hurricane?

By Vicky Sharp

12. In the English football league, how many different suffixes are used in club names?

By Jeanette Jet Alvey-question for her daughter Aimee who is obsessed with zebras (she has about 50!):

13. What is the collective noun of zebras?

Question for her other daughter Ruby:

14. What is the collective noun for tigers?

By Rebecca Ford Page

15. In what year did John Lewis release their first annual Christmas TV advert?

By Natalieanne O'Brien

16. Who is the only person to have eaten 100% British-grown cocoa in the form of a chocolate bar?

By Karen Elsbury Q

17. Where in the UK were the first postcodes introduced?

By Louise Hazel

18. In an adult human, what percentage of bones are in the feet?

By Julie Derbyshire

19. What is the variety of banana that is grown in Derbyshire?

By Paul Haggie

20. What does B&Q stand for? (The DIY shop)

By Rachel Ann Wilson

21. Which poet is buried upright in Westminster Abbey, London, England?

By Neil Britton

22. What animal is the symbol of the 7th Armoured Division (Desert Rats)?

By Darcie Hammett

23. On a navy ship, what are the toilets known as?

By Suzanna Allen

24. In which month is Beaujolais Nouveau released for drinking?

By Chris Trapmore

25. In the Bond films, what is the character name Q short for?

By Charlotte Myall question from her grandad

26. What are the prongs on a fork called?

By Adrian Bull

27. Which bestselling UK number one single has lyrics which don't contain any word from the title of the song but which include the full title of the song which succeeded it at the top of the U.K. singles chart?

By Karen Connolly

28. In Strictly Come Dancing, who is the only professional dancer to have won the Glitter Ball twice?

By Ali Thompson

29. What is the plastic/metal end of a shoelace called?

By Adrian Bull

30. What is the more common name of the symbol technically known as an octothorpe?

By Jackie Howard

31. Who or what is The Old Lady of Threadneedle Street?

By Ian Tucker

32. Before Mount Everest was discovered, what was the highest mountain on Earth?

By Shane Allen

33. Purple Dragon, White Satin & Bolero are varieties of which popular vegetable?

By Juliet Mancey Cornish

34. What was San Francisco called before it was called San Francisco?

By Debbie Rodriguez

35. What was the first advert shown when Channel 5 launched on 30th March 1997?

By Kim Perrie

36. What is Barbara Millicent Roberts better known as?

By Janet Rourke

37. How many boroughs are there in New York City?

By Carol Bucknall

38. What is the collective noun for a group of ladybirds?

By Mark Whitfield

39. Played by Harrison Ford, what is Henry Jones Junior better known as?

By Alison Jane

40. What currency/coins were melted down to make the Rugby Union's Calcutta Cup?

By Colin Fern

41. Which character spoke the first words in the first episode of EastEnders?

By Gilly Erica

42. How many of Shakespeare's plays are set in Italy?

By Claire Anderson-Byrne

43. In the TV series Dallas, who shot JR?

By Liz Howard

44. What are all the female names in the song Mambo No. 5?

By Karen 'Clements' Aulsberry

45. What is the art or practice of bell ringing called?

By Mark Edwards

46. What are the two moons of Mars called?

By Kim Reynolds

47. What is a pangram?

By Claire Louise

48. What were the first ice hockey pucks made out of?

By Jasmine Mason

49. How many hearts does an earth worm have?

By Paul Talmey

50. Where would you find the Islets of Langerhans?

By Alan Jackson

51. What is the stage name of the singer Anna Mae Bullock?

Quiz 1

ROUND 1:
SCIENCE AND NATURE

1. Liver

2. 2

3. 71%

4. Africa

5. Sir Timothy Berners-Lee

6. 2003

7. Zip

8. 212 degrees Fahrenheit

9. Albatross

10. Hydrogen

ROUND 2:
TV AND FILM

1. 4

2. Steve Coogan

3. Jennifer Aniston

4. Crystal Maze

5. Ant and Dec's Saturday Night Takeaway

6. Iain Stirling

7. Hedwig

8. Lost Voice Guy

9. Eddard "Ned" Stark

10. Christopher Lloyd

ROUND 3: MUSIC

1. Bob The Builder

2. Greatest Hits By Queen

3. Someone You Loved

4. Starship

5. Australia

6. You Really Got Me

7. Rocket Man

8. London

9. Will Young

10. Shape of You

ROUND 4: HISTORY

1. 1961

2. 1994

3. 1940

4. 1999

5. 1982

6. 1993

7. 1958

8. 1953

9. 2012

10. 1918

ROUND 5:
GEBERAL KNOWLEDGE

1. Tottenham Hotspur

2. Backgammon

3. Boris Johnson

4. South Tower, Deansgate Square, Manchester

5. St Andrews

6. Ben Nevis

7. Barry Island

8. The Angel of the North

9. Game Of Thrones

10. 1622 People

ANAGRAM
Idris Elba

CRYPTIC CLUE
King's Cross

LINKS
They were the first four modern Olympics host cities (1896, 1900, 1904, 1908)

Quiz 2

ROUND 1: ENTERTAINMENT

1. Ed Sheeran
2. Manhunt
3. Nativity 3
4. Right Said Fred
5. Spooks
6. Jim Carrey
7. The Young Ones
8. Power Rangers
9. Rydell High
10. Bay City Rollers

ROUND 2: SCIENCE AND NATURE

1. Electro
2. Krypton
3. Border Collie
4. Rubella
5. Animal
6. Alexander Fleming
7. Collarbone
8. Joey
9. Cardiologist
10. Yes

ROUND 3:
FOOD AND DRINK

1. Courgettes

2. Green

3. Fish

4. USA

5. A lift for food

6. A French cheese

7. Gin

8. Spinach

9. Raw

10. Float to the surface

ROUND 4:
SPORT

1. Stoke City

2. Harold

3. Wimbledon

4. Alain Prost

5. Patriots

6. Rugby union

7. 6

8. Ski Jump

9. Cycling

10. Evander Holyfield

ROUND 5:
GEBERAL KNOWLEDGE

1. Hollyoaks

2. Microsoft

3. Macbeth

4. Halved

5. 2009

6. A

7. Universities

8. Autopilot

9. Tim Rice

10. Central Perk

ANAGRAM
The King's Speech

CRYPTIC CLUE
Superdry

LINKS
They have all won the Nobel Peace Prize

Quiz 3

ROUND 1: ENTERTAINMENT

1. Charming
2. Life on Mars
3. Lord Farquaad
4. Adele
5. Ian McShane
6. The Fast and the Furious
7. Girls Aloud
8. Outnumbered
9. Johnny English
10. Don McLean

ROUND 2: SCIENCE AND NATURE

1. Iron
2. Saturn
3. 2
4. The Yeti
5. Killer whale
6. Venus flytrap
7. Red roses
8. Husky
9. Aurora Borealis
10. Gaggle

ROUND 3:
FOOD AND DRINK

1. Bacon

2. Argentina

3. Rice

4. Ultra High Temperature

5. True

6. Sevilla Oranges

7. False

8. Pomegranate

9. Mushrooms

10. Italy

ROUND 4:
SPORT

1. 3

2. Grand National

3. Lewis Hamilton

4. 70 minutes

5. Squash

6. Peter Shilton

7. 22

8. True

9. US Open

10. Biathlon

ROUND 5: GEBERAL KNOWLEDGE

1. Germany

2. Sapphire

3. Eleanor Of Aquitaine

4. Mercury

5. 5

6. Green

7. Hawaii

8. Panama

9. 1965

10. Good intentions

ANAGRAM

Ireland, Dublin

CRYPTIC CLUE

Tinie Tempah

LINKS

They are the four sisters in Little Women by Louisa May Alcott

Quiz 4

ROUND 1:
ENTERTAINEMNT

1. Life
2. Niall Horan
3. The Dukes of Hazzard
4. Toy Story
5. Robson and Jerome
6. Open All Hours
7. Ghostbusters
8. Atomic Kitten
9. Broadchurch
10. Roger Rabbit

ROUND 2:
SCIENCE AND NATURE

1. Atmospheric Pressure
2. Hydrogen
3. Shoulder blade
4. South
5. Pencil
6. D
7. Gibraltar
8. Moons
9. Cow
10. 18

ROUND 3: FOOD AND DRINK

1. Australia
2. True
3. Vodka
4. Albumen
5. Saran wrap
6. Peppermint
7. True
8. 10
9. Cabbage
10. Clove

ROUND 4: SPORT

1. Max Verstappen
2. 26 miles
3. Ice Hockey
4. Sir Stanley Matthews
5. 1500 Metres
6. Wimbledon
7. Piste
8. Snooker
9. The race has been stopped
10. Polo

ROUND 5: GEBERAL KNOWLEDGE

1. Republican

2. Job

3. Right shoulder

4. Sri Lanka

5. Butane

6. 2

7. 12

8. M4

9. Black Widow

10. Study

ANAGRAM
Spice Girls

CRYPTIC CLUE
The Hobbit

LINKS
They are the four main characters in Sex and the City

Quiz 5

ROUND 1: ENTERTAINMENT

1. Bruno Mars
2. News For You
3. The Marvel Cinematic Universe
4. True
5. Davina McCall
6. Fight Club
7. Justin Bieber
8. The Sweeney
9. Alcatraz
10. You Do

ROUND 2: SCIENCE AND NATURE

1. Helium
2. 24 Hours
3. First sitting member of US Congress in Space
4. Feet
5. Ovary
6. Drey
7. Animals
8. Meat
9. Chihuahua
10. Cob

ROUND 3:
FOOD AND DRINK

1. Yes

2. Portugal

3. Julienne

4. Muesli

5. Smorgasbord

6. 2

7. Eggs

8. Vodka

9. Ghee

10. False

ROUND 4:
SPORT

1. World Cup Golden Boot

2. South East

3. Europe

4. Polo

5. Packers

6. Triple Jump

7. Sailing

8. Linford Christie

9. Oche

10. Lord's

ROUND 5:
GEBERAL KNOWLEDGE

1. Greendale

2. September

3. Queen Victoria

4. 7

5. St Paul's Cathedral

6. Minaret

7. 39

8. Honda

9. Bureau

10. Silver

ANAGRAM
Leicester City

CRYPTIC CLUE
Richard Nixon

LINKS
They are the four Gospels of the New Testament

Quiz 6

ROUND 1: ENTERTAINMENT

1. Jazzy Jeff and The Fresh Prince
2. The A-Team
3. Frozen
4. Stars
5. The Bill
6. Harrison Ford
7. Leroy Brown
8. Fawlty Towers
9. Funeral
10. The X -Factor

ROUND 2: SCIENCE AND NATURE

1. Nitrogen
2. C
3. Their Feet
4. Backbone
5. Breathe
6. Gas
7. A Bird
8. Wheat
9. Elephant
10. Crocus

ROUND 3:
FOOD AND DRINK

1. Quality Street

2. Duck

3. Claret

4. Australia

5. Spain

6. Pastry

7. Kebab

8. Brandy

9. True

10. Peanut Butter

ROUND 4:
SPORT

1. Liverpool

2. The Oval

3. Athens

4. 20

5. 3

6. Tiger Woods

7. Black

8. ¼ Mile

9. 3

10. Curling

ROUND 5:
GEBERAL KNOWLEDGE

1. Empire State Building

2. Energy

3. Enid Blyton

4. Belfast

5. 1990

6. The New York World

7. BT Tower

8. Ken

9. VHS

10. Fear of religion
    or God

ANAGRAM
Albatross

CRYPTIC CLUE
Victoria Wood

LINKS
They are the four US
presidents depicted
on Mount Rushmore

Quiz 7

ROUND 1: ENTERTAINMENT

1. Peter Andre
2. The Good Life
3. Mission: Impossible
4. American
5. Britain's Got Talent
6. The Rocky Horror Picture Show
7. Gladrags
8. The Big Bang Theory
9. Ocean's Eleven
10. Kajagoogoo

ROUND 2: SCIENCE AND NATURE

1. The Palatine tonsils
2. Squid
3. Leaves
4. Female
5. Children
6. Den
7. Mass
8. Diurnal
9. No
10. Gums

ROUND 3:
FOOD AND DRINK

1. Vodka
2. Saffron
3. Pea
4. Ice Cream
5. Biscuit
6. Deer
7. Pastry
8. Pig
9. Superior
10. Clay/Tandoor

ROUND 4:
SPORT

1. Wembley
2. Two
3. Michael Vaughan
4. Archery
5. Leeds
6. Orienteering
7. Dolphins
8. Ferrari
9. One point
10. Five

ROUND 5:
GEBERAL KNOWLEDGE

1. Sam

2. Sweetheart

3. Alan Dedicoat

4. Christopher Robin

5. Capricorn

6. Michelangelo

7. Wales

8. Neptune

9. Catherine Parr

10. Asked

ANAGRAM
Emily Brontë

CRYPTIC CLUE
Mary Berry

LINKS
They are all Italian Renaissance artists OR they are the Teenage Mutant Ninja Turtles

Quiz 8

ROUND 1: ENTERTAINMENT

1. Swedish House Mafia
2. Industries
3. Armageddon
4. Avril Lavigne
5. Porridge
6. Moulin Rouge
7. Manchester United
8. Raymond
9. Dirty Dancing
10. A Hero

ROUND 2: SCIENCE AND NATURE

1. Red
2. 12
3. Jupiter
4. Tulip
5. A Pride
6. 5
7. A Nursery or a Gaze
8. Vein
9. Australia
10. Yes

ROUND 3:
FOOD AND DRINK

1. Holland

2. C

3. 6

4. Baked Alaska

5. Three

6. Parmesan

7. Ice

8. Cinnamon

9. Vegetables

10. Yeast

ROUND 4:
SPORT

1. Chelsea

2. None

3. Durham

4. Warrington

5. Caddy

6. Cycling

7. Lonsdale belt

8. Nine

9. Four

10. Broncos

ROUND 5:
GEBERAL KNOWLEDGE

1. High blood pressure

2. Frequency

3. Alpha

4. Fast

5. 15

6. Peanuts

7. Cardiff

8. 500

9. Myopia

10. The Muppets

ANAGRAM
Chris Evert

CRYPTIC CLUE
Swansea

LINKS
They are the four
railway stations on a
UK Monopoly Board

Quiz 9

ROUND 1:
TV AND FILM

1. Dad's Army

2. Rene

3. Chris Evans

4. Spooks

5. Phoebe Waller-Bridge

6. The Martian

7. Billy Elliot

8. Toy Story

9. Nakatomi Plaza

10. Cabaret

ROUND 2:
SPORTS AND LEISURE

1. Jonny Wilkinson

2. July

3. Jack Nicholson

4. 6

5. Oxford and Cambridge

6. Monopoly

7. Michelle Obama

8. Wicked

9. York

10. Cluedo

ROUND 3:
MUSIC

1. Westlife

2. Michael

3. Rihanna

4. A girl

5. Elton John

6. She's Electric

7. Somebody

8. Tina Turner

9. Led Zeppelin

10. Somebody to Love

ROUND 4:
FOOD AND DRINK

1. Aubergine

2. In a pastry crust

3. Skittles

4. Newcastle Brown Ale

5. Paprika

6. Tea

7. Coffee (Espresso), hot milk and chocolate

8. Equal parts of cider and lager

9. It is served as a flat square

10. Juniper berries

ROUND 5:
GEBERAL KNOWLEDGE

1. 9

2. Vatican City

3. WhatsApp

4. Harry Potter and the Goblet of Fire

5. Alcohol

6. Katrina and the Waves

7. True

8. Geneva

9. Grease

10. Noah

ANAGRAM
Theresa May

CRYPTIC CLUE
Bear Grylls

LINKS
They are all types of beetle

Quiz 10

ROUND 1: ENTERTAINMENT

1. History
2. Bel Air
3. The Greatest Showman
4. The Ting Tings
5. Friends
6. George Lazenby
7. Madonna
8. Spiderman
9. Dancer
10. Sister Act

ROUND 2: SCIENCE AND NATURE

1. Forearm
2. Laika
3. Bark
4. Rain/Snow
5. Blood
6. Lithium
7. Tail
8. True
9. The rings
10. Lower back

ROUND 3:
FOOD AND DRINK

1. Plums
2. Herring
3. Rum
4. Choux
5. Melon
6. Kosher
7. Mexico
8. Opal Fruits
9. False
10. 11

ROUND 4:
SPORTS

1. Manchester United
2. Birmingham
3. 1500 Metres
4. Solheim Cup
5. 80 minutes
6. Lewis Hamilton
7. Jack Nicklaus
8. Australia
9. 16
10. Five

ROUND 5: GEBERAL KNOWLEDGE

1. Africa

2. San Marino

3. European

4. Bono

5. Green

6. Ben Nevis

7. Mediterranean

8. Sneezing

9. 1968

10. Ringgit

ANAGRAM
Breaking Bad

CRYPTIC CLUE
Stockholm

LINKS
They are the four main characters in South Park

Quiz 11

ROUND 1: ENTERTAINMENT

1. Lewis Capaldi

2. Peep Show

3. Wreck-it Ralph

4. Little Mix

5. Torchwood

6. Inferno

7. Knowing You

8. Channel 4

9. Steven Spielberg

10. The Sheriff

ROUND 2: SCIENCE AND NATURE

1. Silver

2. Measuring radioactivity

3. Attention

4. Windpipe

5. Hospitals

6. Ostrich

7. Hummingbird

8. The male has a mane

9. Albatross

10. Malaria

ROUND 3:
FOOD AND DRINK

1. Mulled
2. Coca-Cola
3. Wheel
4. Denmark
5. Meringue
6. Marathon
7. Pears
8. Sausages
9. Squid
10. Sturgeon

ROUND 4:
SPORT

1. Alan Shearer
2. Before
3. 4
4. Tottenham Hotspur
5. The Boat Race
6. Figure Skating
7. Canada
8. One
9. Real Madrid
10. The Football World Cup

ROUND 5:
GEBERAL KNOWLEDGE

1. Lose One

2. 19

3. Guernsey

4. Catherine of Aragon

5. Winston Churchill

6. Speed camera

7. Syphilis

8. Love

9. Hat

10. The Thames

ANAGRAM
Peak District

CRYPTIC CLUE
Tuba

LINKS
They arc the first names
of the Marx brothers

Quiz 12

ROUND 1: ENTERTAINMENT

1. Frankie Goes to Hollywood
2. The Inbetweeners
3. The Lost World
4. Survivor
5. Pokemon
6. Kramer
7. Rod Stewart
8. Crystal Maze
9. 53
10. Ricky Martin

ROUND 2: SCIENCE AND NATURE

1. Pacific
2. Horse Chestnut
3. Sir Isaac Newton
4. Gas
5. Hands or fingers
6. Vitamin K
7. Canary
8. 4
9. Hands
10. A Boar

ROUND 3:
FOOD AND DRINK

1. Pink

2. Lamb

3. Maize

4. Red

5. Blackthorn

6. India

7. Vegetable

8. Rice

9. Stuffed

10. The dent inside the base

ROUND 4:
GEOGRAPHY

1. Afghanistan

2. The Humber Bridge

3. Seine

4. Europe

5. The Hudson

6. Easter Island

7. Amsterdam

8. Moscow

9. Pennsylvania

10. Richmond Park

ROUND 5: GEBERAL KNOWLEDGE

1. Magna Carta

2. Australia

3. Nine

4. Truffle

5. Blood

6. Whitehall

7. 1st March

8. Australia

9. Hogwarts

10. Eyes

ANAGRAM

South Kensington

CRYPTIC CLUE

Skyfall

LINKS

They are the four official languages of Switzerland

Quiz 13

ROUND 1: ENTERTAINMENT

1. Fifth Harmony
2. Bodyguard
3. Twist and Shout
4. Car
5. Grange Hill
6. Large
7. Black Eyed Peas
8. Smurfette
9. The Wolf of Wall Street
10. Lady Gaga

ROUND 2: SCIENCE AND NATURE

1. Chlorine
2. Shinbone
3. Oak
4. Ethanol
5. Jenny
6. A Crash
7. True
8. Cub
9. A Murder
10. Bamboo

ROUND 3: FOOD AND DRINK

1. Cheddar

2. Sweet

3. Fish

4. Basil

5. Tubular

6. Aniseed

7. Whisky

8. USA

9. Coconut

10. Rum

ROUND 4: WHO SAID IT

1. Nelson Mandela

2. Mother Teresa

3. Anne Frank

4. Martin Luther King Jr

5. Napoleon Bonaparte

6. George Washington

7. Richard Nixon

8. Isaac Newton

9. Aristotle

10. Neil Armstrong

ROUND 5:
GEBERAL KNOWLEDGE

1. Portugal

2. Sunday

3. Sonnet

4. 4

5. USA

6. Robert Langdon

7. Winston Churchill

8. Cyprus

9. Flying

10. 15

ANAGRAM
Lamborghini

CRYPTIC CLUE
Thinking Out Loud

LINKS
They are the four youngest goalscorers in the history of the English Premier League

Quiz 14

ROUND 1: ENTERTAINMENT

1. Meghan Trainor
2. Being Human
3. Azkaban
4. Kelly
5. Jaime Sommers
6. Now You See Me
7. 10cc
8. Annie
9. Upstairs Downstairs
10. 10

ROUND 2: SCIENCE AND NATURE

1. Neon
2. Skin
3. Goat
4. Penguin
5. Buck
6. Water
7. Crabs
8. Tribe or Troop
9. True
10. Kneecap

ROUND 3:
FOOD AND DRINK

1. France

2. Coffee

3. Black Velvet

4. Potato

5. Alcohol by volume

6. Mozzarella

7. Red Peppers

8. Cooking

9. Orange

10. Serbian Donkey

ROUND 4:
ART AND LITERATURE

1. Agatha Christie

2. Stephen King

3. Paris

4. Mrs Tiggy-winkle

5. Narnia

6. Riverdance

7. April

8. The Louvre

9. Andy Warhol

10. Swimming Pools

ROUND 5:
GEBERAL KNOWLEDGE

1. Carbon

2. Dubai International

3. 4000

4. L'Oréal

5. Colombia

6. Texas

7. No

8. Atlantic Ocean

9. Adultery and treason

10. General

ANAGRAM
Cosmopolitan

CRYPTIC CLUE
Carnation

LINKS
They are the last four monarchs of the United Kingdom (Elizabeth II, George VI, Edward VIII, George V)

Quiz 15

ROUND 1:
SCIENCE AND NATURE

1. Filly

2. Fawn

3. Arachnophobia

4. Oxygen

5. Birds

6. Neck

7. Breathe

8. 8

9. Potassium

10. 2010

ROUND 2:
FOOD AND DRINK

1. On vines

2. Italy

3. Fried/toasted bread

4. 4

5. Tomato

6. Tequila

7. Apple

8. Soya beans

9. Tennessee

10. Ice Cream

ROUND 3: GEOGRAPHY

1. Cambridge
2. 1994
3. Bangladesh
4. Texas
5. Zeebrugge
6. Severn
7. True
8. Indian
9. The Andes
10. Romania

ROUND 4: MOVIE TAGLINES

1. I Am Legend
2. Father of the Bride
3. Ferris Bueller's Day Off
4. Psycho
5. Alien
6. The 40-Year-Old Virgin
7. The Social Network
8. Superman
9. Chicken Run
10. The Graduate

ROUND 5:
GEBERAL KNOWLEDGE

1. Charles De Gaulle

2. 82

3. Nike

4. God

5. The Seeing Eye

6. 1979

7. Sydney

8. Six

9. Planet Hollywood

10. Nintendo

ANAGRAM
Stacey Dooley

CRYPTIC CLUE
Gruffalo

LINKS
They are the four members of The Rolling Stones (Mick Jagger, Keith Richards, Charlie Watts, Ronnie Wood)

Quiz 16

ROUND 1: COMPANY SLOGANS

1. Gillette
2. Burger King
3. Disneyland
4. BMW
5. Maxwell House Coffee
6. EA Sports
7. Rice Krispies
8. McDonald's
9. Maybelline
10. Budweiser

ROUND 2: HISTORY

1. King Harold
2. The Black Death
3. Lancaster
4. 16th
5. James I
6. Duke of Wellington
7. 1837
8. 15th August
9. 1969
10. 2012

ROUND 3:
CAPITAL CITIES

1. Cuba

2. Uganda

3. Uruguay

4. India

5. South Korea

6. Estonia

7. Venezuela

8. Egypt

9. Barbados

10. Slovakia

ROUND 4:
CHEMICAL SYMBOLS

1. Magnesium

2. Argon

3. Silicon

4. Nickel

5. Copper

6. Zinc

7. Palladium

8. Xenon

9. Hafnium

10. Mercury

ROUND 5:
GEBERAL KNOWLEDGE

1. Eros

2. Bucks Fizz

3. Coastline

4. Spice Girls

5. Sean Connery

6. Offshore/Pirate

7. KFC

8. Joe Wicks

9. Black

10. George Bush

ANAGRAM
Potato Masher

CRYPTIC CLUE
Dawn French

LINKS
They are all sports teams based in Los Angeles, USA

Quiz 17

ROUND 1: ENTERTAINMENT

1. Dolittle
2. Bad Boys for Life
3. The Irishman
4. Top Gun
5. Vito Corleone
6. Elisha Cuthbert
7. The Office
8. How I Met Your Mother
9. The A-Team
10. Glee

ROUND 2: SPORT AND LEISURE

1. Uno
2. Dice
3. 28
4. 6
5. Self-Contained Underwater Breathing Apparatus
6. Liverpool, Tottenham, Arsenal and Chelsea
7. Giants
8. Sumo Wrestling
9. Wimbledon
10. Steph Houghton

ROUND 3: MUSIC

1. NSYNC

2. Weird Al Yankovic

3. Zayn Malik

4. The Animals

5. Rapper's Delight

6. 8 – Give You Up, Let You Down, Run Around, Desert You, Make You Cry, Say Goodbye, Tell a Lie, Hurt You

7. Hanson

8. This

9. Lou Bega

10. Elvis Presley

ROUND 4: SCIENCE, NATURE AND TECHNOLOGY

1. Sett

2. Lettuce

3. Space bar

4. Uranium

5. Dolly

6. Red

7. Sound intensity

8. 7

9. TikTok

10. Nebbiolo

ROUND 5:
GEBERAL KNOWLEDGE –
NHS AND CELEBS

1. London

2. 595 and Area car driver

3. Femur

4. 3 awards

5. Skin

6. Grant Shapps

7. 1948

8. The Armstrong and Miller Show

9. Ben Watson

10. Waterfalls

ANAGRAM
Missouri

CRYPTIC CLUE
Winston Churchill

LINKS
They are all types of dove

Quiz 18

ROUND 1: ENTERTAINMENT

1. Ashes to Ashes
2. Claude Littner
3. Noel Edmonds
4. Baz Luhrmann
5. Me
6. (Everything I Do) I Do It For You
7. Bros
8. Close Encounters
9. Arnold Schwarzenegger
10. Top Gun

ROUND 2: SCIENCE AND NATURE

1. Nectar
2. Universal Serial Bus
3. 94
4. Pancreas
5. Chicken
6. Sodium
7. Nerve
8. Plants
9. Tin
10. Iron

ROUND 3:
FOOD AND DRINK

1. A frozen dessert
2. Buck's Fizz
3. 30
4. Spain
5. Deer
6. Green
7. Vodka
8. Leek
9. Plums
10. Tomato

ROUND 4:
SPORT

1. Sheffield United
2. 82
3. Yellow
4. Cricket
5. Scotland
6. Tottenham Hotspur
7. Leeds Rhinos
8. BMW Sauber
9. Middlesex
10. Aintree

ROUND 5:
GEBERAL KNOWLEDGE

1. Joe Biden

2. M

3. Barclays

4. 1948

5. Hey Diddle Diddle

6. Liverpool

7. Panda

8. Byker Grove

9. Venice

10. Motorway

ANAGRAM
Fred Flintstone

CRYPTIC CLUE
Orchid

LINKS
They have all been played by Benedict Cumberbatch

Quiz 19

ROUND 1: MUSIC

1. Queen
2. The Nolans
3. Gerry and the Pacemakers
4. Elton John
5. Tribes
6. The Charlatans
7. t.A.T.u
8. Bastille
9. Girls Aloud
10. I Can

ROUND 2: HISTORY

1. Portugal
2. The Great Fire of London
3. Mary Queen of Scots
4. Battle of Balaclava
5. United Kingdom
6. Thomas Cook
7. Test tube baby
8. Margaret Bondfield
9. Iranian
10. Canada

ROUND 3:
CHEMICAL SYMBOLS

1. Phosphorus
2. Cobalt
3. Manganese
4. Gallium
5. Arsenic
6. Zirconium
7. Indium
8. Tin
9. Cerium
10. Tungsten

ROUND 4:
COMPANY SLOGANS

1. Adidas
2. Capital One
3. Coca-Cola
4. Mastercard
5. KitKat
6. Heinz
7. Ronseal
8. Audi
9. Marmite
10. Heineken

ROUND 5:
GEBERAL KNOWLEDGE

1. Hermes

2. Air

3. Cotton

4. USA

5. Books

6. Knight

7. Sapphire

8. Hawaii

9. Revelation

10. James Bond

ANAGRAM
National Geographic

CRYPTIC CLUE
Chrysler

LINKS
They are the four US states that border Mexico

Quiz 20

ROUND 1: MOVIES

1. James Cameron
2. Donald Glover
3. Rupert Grint
4. Minions
5. Brie Larson
6. Star Wars
7. Mike Myers
8. Jurassic Park
9. Rain Man
10. Elliott

ROUND 2: CHEMICAL SYMBOLS

1. Pb
2. Rd
3. Po
4. U
5. Hf
6. V
7. Au
8. Hg
9. Pt
10. Hs

ROUND 3:
HISTORY

1. Lord Nelson

2. Titanic

3. William Pitt the Younger

4. Clive Sinclair

5. Periodic Table

6. 15th

7. Karl Donitz

8. Pompeii

9. Lee Harvey Oswald

10. William Shakespeare

ROUND 4:
COMPANY SLOGANS

1. John Lewis

2. Compare the Market

3. Honda

4. Halifax

5. HSBC

6. B&Q

7. Cadburys Crème Egg

8. Red Bull

9. Specsavers

10. Argos

ROUND 5:
GEBERAL KNOWLEDGE

1. Fertility and marriage

2. Definition

3. Lincolnshire

4. Germany

5. Strangers or foreigners

6. Amethyst

7. Trouble

8. 12

9. 220

10. Metal Gear

ANAGRAM
West Side Story

CRYPTIC CLUE
Sue Barker

LINKS
They were the last four UK prime ministers before Johnson (Blair, Brown, Cameron, May)

Quiz 21

ROUND 1: TV AND FILM

1. 1998

2. The Avengers

3. Only Fools and Horses

4. The X-Files

5. The Greatest Dancer

6. 1965

7. The Goonies

8. The Shawshank Redemption

9. Snatch

10. Titanic

ROUND 2: SPORT

1. 155: Player fouls and leaves white in a position that would allow opposing player to call free ball

2. Australia

3. 7

4. Leicester City

5. Italy or Scotland

6. 1988

7. Old Trafford

8. US Open

9. Brawn GP

10. Tiger Roll

ROUND 3: MUSIC

1. Tom Jones
2. Buttercup
3. Boney M
4. YMCA
5. Bon Jovi
6. David Bowie
7. The Mickey Mouse Club
8. Billie Piper
9. Craig David
10. Dance Monkey

ROUND 4: GEOGRAPHY

1. Bristol
2. India
3. Eiffel Tower, 324m – 158m
4. John O'Groats
5. 5: Italy, France, Germany, Austria, Liechtenstein
6. Folkestone
7. 6
8. Cuba
9. 2: Alaska and Hawaii
10. Gibraltar City

ROUND 5: GEBERAL KNOWLEDGE

1. 8

2. Snapchat

3. Hilda

4. William Shakespeare

5. 14th century: 1350

6. Catherine Parr

7. 21

8. Ukraine

9. 2020

10. Tesla

ANAGRAM

Willy Wonka

CRYPTIC CLUE

Warren Street

LINKS

They have all won 'I'm a Celebrity… Get Me Out Of Here!'

Quiz 22

ROUND 1: TV AND FILM

1. I Got You Babe
2. Stephen Fry
3. Chicago
4. Jess
5. 22
6. Ned Stark
7. The Taming of the Shrew
8. Jason
9. Blue
10. The Winchester

ROUND 2: SPORT AND LEISURE

1. Chess
2. 5
3. Mayfair
4. High Jump
5. 7
6. Rowing, Tug of war
7. 37
8. Curling
9. Hedgehog
10. Mah-jong

ROUND 3:
MUSIC

1. Westlife

2. Arctic Monkeys

3. Destiny's Child

4. Barbie

5. Wannabe

6. Mr Blobby

7. Coldplay

8. Radio 1

9. The Sunshine Band

10. The names of the song are not mentioned in the song

ROUND 4:
SCIENCE AND NATURE

1. 4

2. Hydrogen

3. 8

4. Feet

5. 6

6. False

7. Earth

8. -40

9. Gold

10. Strawberry

ROUND 5:
GEBERAL KNOWLEDGE

1. 10

2. Norway

3. 4

4. Australia

5. Mark Wallinger

6. USA

7. Tesla

8. Andrew Lloyd Webber

9. £20

10. Samaritans

ANAGRAM
Katherine Ryan

CRYPTIC CLUE
Timberland

LINKS
They are all David Bowie characters

Quiz 23

ROUND 1: MUSIC

1. Ozzy Osbourne

2. NSYNC

3. Isaac Hayes

4. Especially For You

5. Shakespears Sister

6. Rednex

7. Spirit in the Sky

8. Amy Winehouse

9. 1995

10. Save Your Kisses for Me

ROUND 2: HISTORY

1. Charles II

2. Manchester United

3. US House of Representatives

4. Tallest Building in the World

5. The Old Bailey

6. July

7. New Zealand

8. Prime Minister

9. Bayeux Tapestry

10. Fidel Castro

ROUND 3:
COMPANY SLOGANS

1. T-Mobile
2. Vodafone
3. George Foreman Grill
4. Max Factor
5. Olay
6. Whiskas
7. Sure
8. Lindt
9. Dolmio
10. Sainsbury's

ROUND 4:
MOVIES

1. Endgame
2. Leonardo Di Caprio
3. Vin Diesel
4. Daniel Craig
5. John McClane
6. Robin Williams
7. Olivia Colman
8. Apollo Creed
9. Kenickie Murdoch
10. Jaws

ROUND 5:
GEBERAL KNOWLEDGE

1. Scene

2. Israel

3. Clocks

4. St James' Park

5. January

6. Ox

7. Matthew

8. Wife

9. Pandora

10. Grand Theft Auto V

ANAGRAM
Rocky Mountains

CRYPTIC CLUE
Mamma Mia

LINKS
They are (as of 2020) the last four winners of the English Football League Championship

Quiz 24

ROUND 1: MOVIES

1. George Lucas

2. Idina Menzel

3. Lord of the Rings

4. Joker

5. Pirates of the Caribbean

6. Bill Pullman

7. Sid

8. Terminator 2

9. Ghost

10. Top Gun

ROUND 2: NAME THE MANUFACTURER

1. Ariel

2. Seat

3. Mazda

4. Honda

5. Nissan

6. Volkswagen

7. Audi

8. Jaguar

9. Land Rover

10. Hyundai

ROUND 3:
HISTORY

1. November

2. Edward VII

3. Zimbabwe

4. USA

5. No

6. Monday

7. New Zealand

8. Barrow

9. The Victoria Cross

10. Lady Godiva

ROUND 4:
UK TOURIST ATTRACTIONS
WHICH COUNTY?

1. Wiltshire

2. West Yorkshire

3. Lancashire

4. Tyne and Wear

5. Shire of Inverness

6. Somerset

7. Cornwall

8. West Midlands

9. Somerset

10. Cheshire

ROUND 5: GEBERAL KNOWLEDGE

1. War
2. Light
3. Hawaii
4. Small things
5. April
6. Scout
7. Phone
8. 121
9. Barbie
10. EA Sports

ANAGRAM

Raheem Sterling

CRYPTIC CLUE

Newcastle

LINKS

They are all members of Coldplay

Quiz 25

ROUND 1: MUSIC

1. Debbie Harry
2. The Kinks
3. My Baby
4. Tainted
5. No Limit
6. A Bad Day
7. The Deep
8. Farrokh Bulsara
9. David Sneddon
10. Love City Groove

ROUND 2: GEOGRAPHY

1. Michigan
2. Argentina
3. Seven
4. Kentucky
5. 3000
6. Iran
7. Canada
8. Indonesia
9. Southampton
10. Portugal

ROUND 3:
HISTORY

1. D-Day
2. Edward VIII
3. Bronze Age
4. Boston
5. Government
6. King Arthur
7. Harvard
8. The White House
9. 15th Century
10. War of the Worlds

ROUND 4:
CONNECTIONS ROUND

1. Bat (Man)
2. (Flash) Gordon
3. Quicksilver
4. Winter (Soldier)
5. Storm
6. (Rocket) Racoon
7. Spider (Man)
8. Captain (America/ Marvel)
9. Iron (Man)
10. All Superheroes

ROUND 5:
GEBERAL KNOWLEDGE

1. Flowers

2. Stock

3. Lebanon

4. Insects

5. May

6. Exodus

7. Deaf

8. Lara Croft

9. Plastic at the end of the shoe lace

10. Polaroid

ANAGRAM
Crocodile

CRYPTIC CLUE
Eamonn Holmes

LINKS
They fought as allies (known collectively as the Central Powers) in World War One

Quiz 26

ROUND 1: ACRONYMS

1. Space
2. Lettuce
3. Quotations
4. Shanghai
5. Quotient
6. Automatic
7. International
8. Tactics
9. Water Displacement
10. Young

ROUND 2: MOVIES

1. Richard Curtis
2. Edward Lewis
3. Pretty in Pink
4. Groundhog Day
5. Cuba Gooding Jr
6. Smith
7. Wedding Singer
8. Mamma Mia
9. Enchanted
10. The Beatles

ROUND 3:
TV

1. Bart Simpson
2. Rodney Trotter
3. Top Gear
4. Casualty
5. Gilmore Girls
6. Baywatch
7. Birds of a Feather
8. The Saint
9. Donnelly
10. Torquay

ROUND 4:
SPORT

1. 1986
2. Murray
3. India
4. Pole Vault
5. Scottish
6. 3 points
7. Pawns
8. Sir Henry Cooper
9. Rugby union
10. Darts

ROUND 5:
GEBERAL KNOWLEDGE

1. Bavarian

2. France

3. Julian

4. Illness

5. March

6. Malachi

7. Daisy

8. £500

9. Jersey

10. Ricky Wilson

ANAGRAM
Ed Sheeran

CRYPTIC CLUE
Poker Face

LINKS
They are the first names of the Brontë siblings

Quiz 27

ROUND 1: GEOGRAPHY

1. Spanish
2. Saudi Arabia
3. Russia
4. Lake Erie
5. Peru
6. The Congo
7. Isle of Wight
8. Chile
9. Georgia
10. Lyon

ROUND 2: GUESS THE YEAR

1. 1605
2. 1694
3. 1894
4. 1922
5. 1952
6. 1973
7. 1989
8. 1997
9. 1903
10. 1944

ROUND 3: HISTORY

1. Germany
2. Bronze Age
3. Tower of London
4. Pacific
5. Neville Chamberlain
6. 116 years
7. Stephen
8. Dead Sea Scrolls
9. Jack the Ripper
10. Dynamite

ROUND 4: TV

1. Jenny Ryan
2. Downton Abbey
3. Killing Eve
4. Barbara Knox
5. Cheers
6. The Great British Bake Off
7. Not Going Out
8. Jimmy Carr
9. Bartholomew JoJo Simpson
10. Fraggle Rock

ROUND 5:
GEBERAL KNOWLEDGE

1. Religion

2. Kilt

3. Tourist Trophy

4. 10 Yards

5. Abbey Road

6. ALS

7. Portable document format

8. Lattice

9. The Dark Destroyer

10. Ireland

ANAGRAM
The Tempest

CRYPTIC CLUE
Citroën

LINKS
They are all Beyoncé singles

Quiz 28

ROUND 1:
MUSIC

1. The Pretenders
2. TLC
3. Lonnie Donegan
4. I Love You
5. Top Gun
6. Will Smith
7. Eric Prydz
8. Plain white T's
9. Calum Scott
10. Katrina and the Waves

ROUND 2:
ART AND LITERATURE

1. King Lear
2. Sea
3. Casino Royale
4. 13¾
5. Frog
6. Peter Pan
7. John Milton
8. Susan Hill
9. Spider
10. Laureate

ROUND 3:
NAME THE MANUFACTURER

1. Porsche
2. Toyota
3. Smart
4. Saab
5. Dodge
6. Chevrolet
7. Ford
8. Lotus
9. Infiniti
10. Kia

ROUND 4:
SPORT

1. Abide With Me
2. Wrestling
3. Pool
4. Ice
5. Jimmy White
6. American Football
7. 4.25
8. Ice Hockey
9. Oliver McCall
10. Matthew Webb

ROUND 5:
GEBERAL KNOWLEDGE

1. £60

2. Stephen Fry

3. M6

4. The Who

5. District of Columbia

6. Crystal Palace Transmitter

7. 24

8. Lord Grantham

9. Edinburgh

10. Paw Patrol

ANAGRAM
Barcelona

CRYPTIC CLUE
Maple

LINKS
They are all Ancient Greek gods

Quiz 29

ROUND 1: MUSIC

1. Led Zeppelin
2. Chubby Checker
3. Dr Hook
4. Up
5. Gangsta's Paradise
6. Michelle McManus
7. Pharrell Williams
8. Cliff Richard
9. Gina G
10. Hear'Say

ROUND 2: SPORT

1. Tottenham Hotspur
2. 6
3. 4
4. London Broncos
5. Clay
6. Weightlifting
7. Polka dot (red and white)
8. 1997
9. Six
10. 300

ROUND 3:
HISTORY

1. Russia
2. The Home Guard
3. Donald Trump
4. Elizabeth I
5. The Salvation Army
6. 17th March
7. Spanish
8. Hyde Park
9. Wallis Simpson
10. 1950s

ROUND 4:
CAPITAL CITIES

1. Australia
2. Kenya
3. Malta
4. North Korea
5. Poland
6. Indonesia
7. Hungary
8. Cyprus
9. Croatia
10. Canada

ROUND 5:
GERBERAL KNOWLEDGE

1. Earthquakes

2. Belgium

3. Little Mix

4. Goal Attack

5. Gru

6. Millennium Dome

7. Bob the Builder

8. The Sun

9. Glastonbury

10. There isn't one

ANAGRAM
Some Like It Hot

CRYPTIC CLUE
Beatrix Potter

LINKS
They are all male pen names used by female authors (J.K. Rowling, Mary Ann Evans, Ann Rule, Emily Brontë)

Quiz 30

ROUND 1: TV

1. Lip Sync Battle
2. Gotham
3. The Love Lift
4. Brendan Sheerin
5. Gordon Ramsay
6. The Thin Blue Line
7. Baywatch
8. Victoria Wood
9. The Bill
10. Dad's Army

ROUND 2: SPORT

1. Premier League
2. Graham Hill
3. No
4. Clive Woodward
5. French Open
6. White
7. Southpaw
8. Slate
9. Eight
10. Sub-four-minute mile

ROUND 3:
GUESS THE YEAR

1. 1975

2. 1979

3. 1982

4. 1990

5. 1996

6. 1984

7. 1940

8. 2010

9. 1966

10. 1945

ROUND 4:
MOVIE TAGLINES

1. Bad Teacher

2. Catch Me If You Can

3. The First Wives Club

4. Grosse Pointe Blank

5. Liar Liar

6. Mars Attacks

7. Monsters Inc

8. Monty Python and the Holy Grail

9. Shaun of the Dead

10. There's Something About Mary

ROUND 5:
GEBERAL KNOWLEDGE

1. Woody

2. Birmingham

3. Recognition

4. David Jason

5. Cluedo

6. Joe Lycett

7. Hansel and Gretel

8. Italy

9. Isle of Man

10. Iron Man

ANAGRAM
Ainsley Harriott

CRYPTIC CLUE
Gloucester Road

LINKS
They are the host countries for the four annual tennis Grand Slam tournaments

Quiz 31

ROUND 1: MUSIC

1. Steven Tyler
2. Backstreet Boys
3. Elvis Presley
4. Alice Cooper
5. Black Box
6. The Lightning Seeds
7. Peter Kay
8. Journey
9. Calvin Harris
10. Eurovision

ROUND 2: CAPITALS

1. Norway
2. Tunisia
3. Trinidad & Tobago
4. Syria
5. Switzerland
6. South Korea
7. Sierra Leone
8. Russia
9. Nepal
10. New Zealand

ROUND 3:
HISTORY

1. Germany

2. Michael Collins

3. Anne Boleyn

4. 1960

5. Enigma

6. Parker

7. Atomic Bomb

8. 14th Century

9. Marilyn Monroe

10. Delaware

ROUND 4:
ART AND LITERATURE

1. Joanne

2. Mycroft

3. Mario Puzo

4. Arthur

5. Barack Obama

6. Van Gogh

7. St Paul's

8. Cassius Marcellus Coolidge

9. Sparrow

10. London

ROUND 5: GEBERAL KNOWLEDGE

1. Grandpa Shark

2. Wicked

3. Scooby-Doo

4. Danube

5. Poker

6. Gamma

7. Gnasher

8. A4

9. Modulation

10. June

ANAGRAM

Emma Thompson

CRYPTIC CLUE

Dunfermline

LINKS

They are the four members of Queen

Quiz 32

ROUND 1: MUSIC

1. Boyzone
2. Dave Grohl
3. I Got You Babe
4. Queen
5. Barbara Dickson
6. Robert Miles
7. Shane Ward
8. Billie Eilish
9. Five
10. The Bee Gees

ROUND 2: GUESS THE YEAR

1. 1974
2. 1976
3. 1983
4. 1986
5. 1997
6. 1894
7. 1963
8. 1976
9. 1910
10. 1776

ROUND 3:
TV

1. Kevin Bishop

2. Rock and Chips

3. Derren Brown

4. The West Wing

5. Saved by the Bell

6. The X-Files

7. World War II

8. Hot Mum

9. Thomas the Tank Engine

10. Shameless

ROUND 4:
SPORT

1. 9

2. 1994

3. 0

4. 2

5. Switzerland

6. Baton

7. Red Rum

8. Snooker

9. Gold

10. Baseball

ROUND 5:
GEBERAL KNOWLEDGE

1. Corsica

2. The Volga

3. The Television

4. £120

5. Quiver

6. Alan Freeman

7. 1960

8. Apollo

9. Philadelphia

10. Deadly Nightshade

ANAGRAM
Horse Chestnut

CRYPTIC CLUE
Vans

LINKS
They were all US presidents who were assassinated while in office

Quiz 33

ROUND 1: NAME THE MANUFACTURER

1. Vauxhall
2. Abarth
3. Maserati
4. Isuzu
5. Rolls Royce
6. Suzuki
7. Subaru
8. Peugeot
9. Lamborghini
10. Bentley

ROUND 2: SPORT

1. Third Place
2. Canadian
3. 50
4. Martin
5. American
6. Red
7. Green
8. Scottish
9. 800 Metres
10. Table tennis

ROUND 3:
TV

1. Game of Thrones
2. Kiefer Sutherland
3. Ultimate Force
4. The Vicar of Dibley
5. Scrubs
6. Family Guy
7. Anyway
8. The Two Ronnies
9. Red Dwarf
10. Empire

ROUND 4:
GEOGRAPHY

1. Damascus
2. Alaska
3. Saudi Arabia
4. Brazil
5. K2
6. Africa
7. Etna
8. Malaysia
9. The Strait of Gibraltar
10. Sahara

ROUND 5:
GEBERAL KNOWLEDGE

1. Methane

2. £180

3. Mansion House

4. Colony

5. 24

6. Playing Cards

7. Ant

8. Orchid

9. Marchioness

10. Sirius A

ANAGRAM
Sherlock Holmes

CRYPTIC CLUE
Despicable Me

LINKS
They are the four English counties that border Wales

Quiz 34

ROUND 1: MUSIC

1. Gwen Stefani
2. The Beatles
3. Summertime
4. Three
5. China
6. Celine Dion
7. Button
8. One Direction
9. Pop Idol
10. Engelbert Humperdink

ROUND 2: SPORT

1. Premier League
2. Australia
3. Both/2
4. 5
5. 4
6. Wigan Warriors
7. Eric Bristow
8. 100 Metres Hurdles
9. Boxing
10. 2

ROUND 3:
TV

1. Top Gear
2. Sunday Brunch
3. Shield
4. Tom Hanks
5. Breaking Bad
6. The Big Bang Theory
7. Holby
8. Nelson Mandela House
9. Born
10. The Two Ronnies

ROUND 4:
ART AND LITERATURE

1. Othello
2. Upstage
3. Spain and or Portugal
4. Sculpture
5. Alexander Dumas
6. Judas Iscariot
7. Anne Hathaway
8. Pierre-Auguste Renoir
9. The Satanic Verses
10. A male ballet dancer

ROUND 5:
GEBERAL KNOWLEDGE

1. Mormons

2. Marionette

3. Coca-Cola

4. Kappa

5. Egypt

6. 5

7. TNT

8. Nosebleed

9. Malcolm X

10. Kidney

ANAGRAM
Grand Theft Auto

CRYPTIC CLUE
Jailhouse Rock

LINKS
They are all sequels in the Ice Age franchise

Quiz 35

ROUND 1: MUSIC

1. UK
2. Cilla Black
3. Nothing
4. The One and Only
5. The River
6. Believe in Me
7. The Beach Boys
8. Orange
9. Carl Douglas
10. Stars In Their Eyes

ROUND 2: SPORT

1. Gareth Southgate
2. Michael Schumacher
3. 5
4. Martina Navratilova
5. Tim Henman
6. The Masters
7. The goalkeeper
8. 6
9. 50 Metres
10. Melbourne

ROUND 3:
TV

1. Intelligence
2. Martin Freeman
3. Things
4. State Of Play
5. Hugh Laurie
6. Friends
7. Live and Kicking
8. Bernard's Watch
9. Sabrina the Teenage Witch
10. The Young Ones

ROUND 4:
GEOGRAPHY

1. USA (Hawaii)
2. Asia
3. Tokyo
4. 6
5. Africa
6. Mexico
7. Azerbaijan
8. Switzerland
9. Greece
10. Iberian

ROUND 5: GEBERAL KNOWLEDGE

1. Carbon

2. Forehead

3. Helmut Kohl

4. Tamagotchi

5. Marie Curie

6. Green

7. Pigs in Blankets

8. Delta

9. South Park

10. Fog

ANAGRAM

Parsley

CRYPTIC CLUE

Piano

LINKS

They are the four members of The Monkees

Readers' Round Answers

1. You Can't Hurry Love by Phil Collins

2. Switzerland

3. The Boys' Brigade in 1883 (the Scouts was an offshoot by Baden-Powell in the early 1900s)

4. Pink

5. No sunlight, don't get wet and no food after midnight.

6. Etched around the edge of a £2 coin.

7. Bacon (BAcON)

8. Snakes

9. Asparagus

10. 775

11. 12

12. 19

13. Dazzle, Herd or Zeal

14. Ambush or streak

15. 2007

16. Queen Elizabeth II when she was a princess.

17. Norwich, in 1959

18. 25%

19. Cavendish banana grown at Chatsworth.

20. Block & Quayle

21. Ben Jonson. He told the Dean of Westminster that two feet by two feet would do for him as he was poor.

22. Jerboa

23. The Head

24. November

25. Quartermaster

26. Tines

27. Bohemian Rhapsody (which was succeeded as no 1 by Mamma Mia).

28. Aliona Vilani (with Harry Judd and Jay McGuinness)

29. An aglet

30. Hashtag (sometimes called the "pound sign" in the US)

31. The Bank of England

32. Mount Everest

33. Carrot

34. Yerba Buena

35. Chanel No. 5

36. Barbie

37. 5: Queens, Manhattan, Bronx, Brooklyn, Staten Island

38. Loveliness

39. Indiana Jones

40. Rupee

41. Dennis Watts

42. There are 38 plays and 13 are set in Italy.

43. Kristin Shepard

44. Jessica, Monica, Rita, Sandra, Tina, Mary, Erica, Angela, Pamela

45. Campanology

46. Phobos and Deimos

47. A sentence containing all the letters of the alphabet

48. Frozen cow dung

49. 5

50. In the pancreas

51. Tina Turner

Notes

Notes

Notes

Charities and Support

Jay's Virtual Pub Quiz has worked with many charities over the weeks, but we wanted to highlight these four and encourage you to make your own donations and support.

NHS Charities Together is a collective experience representing, supporting and championing the work of the NHS's official charities. This was the first charity we worked with and it raised nearly £200k for them, which stands as one of their biggest fundraisers. As the quiz started after the NHS clap for carers, this was the perfect charity choice for a number of weeks. Donate: www.justgiving.com/originalvirtualpubquiz

The Connection at St Martin's helps thousands of people every year to move away from, and stay off, the streets of London. This charity supported Jay during his time of need. www.justgiving.com/virtualpubquizcstm

The Diana Award is a living legacy to Princess Diana's belief that young people have the power to change the world for the better. Alex works there as Deputy CEO, and we supported their anti-bullying programme, after Alex told me about his own experience of bullying when he was younger. www.justgiving.com/virtualpubquiz2

Alzheimer's Research UK is the UK's leading dementia research charity, dedicated to causes, diagnosis, prevention, treatment and cure. We have helped this charity raise over £300,000 with one night alone hosted by Stephen Fry raising £200,000! As a result we went on to run a series of Friday takeovers with, the likes of Jonathan Ross and Scarlett Moffat hosting. www.justgiving.com/virtualpubquizaruk

#JaysVirtualPubQuiz is live from 19:50 BST on Thursdays and Saturdays for a 20:15 quiz start time, and specialist pre-records are uploaded almost daily!

youtube.com/TheVirtualPubQuiz

facebook.com/JaysVirtualPubQuiz

twitter.com/TheVirtualPubQ1 @TheVirtualPubQ1

instagram.com/thevirtualpubquiz/ @TheVirtualPubQuiz

Website: jaysvirtualpubquiz.com

Support Jay by becoming a member:
www.patreon.com/thevirtualpubquiz

Get your merchandise at:
jays-virtual-pub-quiz.teemill.com and prezzybox.com/jay

Thank yous

Firstly, to my wife Sarah for always believing in all of my ideas no matter how crazy they are, and for always having faith in me.

To Alex Holmes. It feels like we have been friends for more than just a matter of months. You are an incredible human being working tirelessly to make this whole thing as successful as it has been, lifting me up through those moments when things were tough and keeping the faith and believing in me. I can never thank you enough for what you have done.

To my quiz team (it's my book, I'm calling us that!): you guys know who you are so I'm not going to name you all individually (I'd never hear the end of it!) But for all our Thursday night laughs and Friday morning hangovers, look where we are now! Thank you for being a great group to go out and have a laugh with.

To my friends, thank you. I'm proud to know I have friends like you. Truly one for every possible scenario!

To my family, thank you for always believing in me, and for the advice, support and keeping me grounded.

To the team at Mirror Books, Ajda, Kaz and Mel: thank you. I have never had to do anything like this before and I know you are used to working with established professional authors, not this idiot! I'm sorry for all the sleepless nights, but thank you for all your support and guidance.

To the charities: The Connection at St Martin's, The Diana Award, Alzheimer's Research UK, NHS Charities together, and all of the other charities we have supported and showcased. Having seen first hand what you and your teams do, we are truly grateful for all the hard work you have done to make each of your featured charities moments as successful as you could.

And finally to the community, from Patreons, Instagram, Twitter and Facebook. Without your support and your messages none of this would have been possible. I cannot thank you all enough, and hopefully we will all play a quiz together one day!